THE
MARRIAGE
CORPORATION

Corporate Strategies for Fulfilling God's
Purpose in a Covenant Marriage

DR. RICHARD SERRANO
DR. NEPHETINA SERRANO

WESTBOW
PRESS®
A DIVISION OF THOMAS NELSON
& ZONDERVAN

Unless otherwise stated, scripture taken from the King James Version of the Bible. Scripture quotations marked (NIV) are taken from the Holy Bible, New International Version®, NIV®. Copyright © 1973, 1978, 1984, 2011 by Biblica, Inc.™ Used by permission of Zondervan. All rights reserved worldwide. www. zondervan.com The "NIV" and "New International Version" are trademarks registered in the United States Patent and Trademark Office by Biblica, Inc.™

This book is a work of non-fiction. Unless otherwise noted, the author and the publisher make no explicit guarantees as to the accuracy of the information contained in this book and in some cases, names of people and places have been altered to protect their privacy.

WestBow Press books may be ordered through booksellers or by contacting:

WestBow Press
A Division of Thomas Nelson & Zondervan
1663 Liberty Drive
Bloomington, IN 47403
www.westbowpress.com
1 (866) 928-1240

Because of the dynamic nature of the Internet, any web addresses or links contained in this book may have changed since publication and may no longer be valid. The views expressed in this work are solely those of the author and do not necessarily reflect the views of the publisher, and the publisher hereby disclaims any responsibility for them.

Any people depicted in stock imagery provided by Getty Images are models, and such images are being used for illustrative purposes only. Certain stock imagery © Getty Images.

ISBN: 978-1-9736-3265-8 (sc)
ISBN: 978-1-9736-3266-5 (hc)
ISBN: 978-1-9736-3264-1 (e)

Library of Congress Control Number: 2018909072

Print information available on the last page.

WestBow Press rev. date: 03/21/2019

Contents

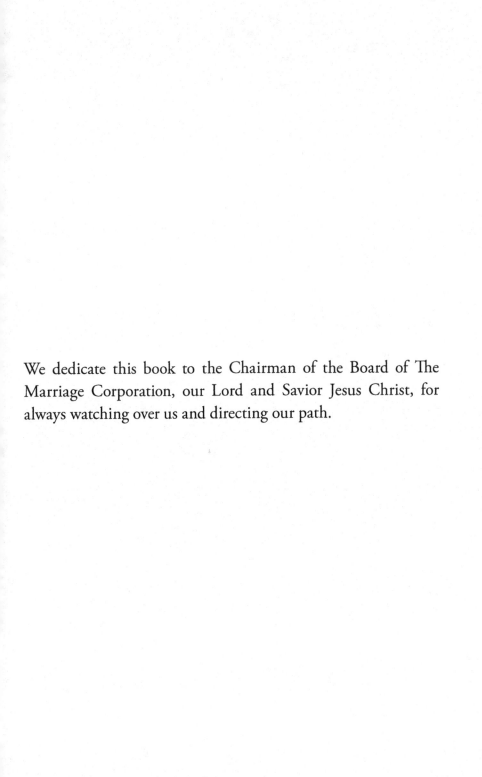

We dedicate this book to the Chairman of the Board of The Marriage Corporation, our Lord and Savior Jesus Christ, for always watching over us and directing our path.

Acknowledgments

To our parents, the late Esteban and Rosa Maria Serrano, Roosevelt Brant Jr. and Emma Jean Brant. Thank you for laying the foundation of order and discipline in the home, for teaching us how to care for ourselves, and for showing us the value of working together as a family, we are forever grateful for the love you have demonstrated to us.

To our friend who worked with us on this project, His Excellency Yomi Garnett, MD, UN-affiliated Universal Peace Federation Ambassador for Peace, we cannot adequately express the level of gratitude and appreciation we have for our heavenly Father in sending you to us at just the right time. Thank you for all the hard work and dedication to seeing this project to completion.

To our overseer; Father and Mother in the gospel; Bishop Ernest C. Morris Sr., and Mother Winifred Morris at Mt. Airy Church of God in Christ, have led us by example for over twenty-five years, and we are truly thankful to you for being living examples for us to follow. Thank you for always encouraging us to live out our destiny.

To our amazing and most accomplished professional photographer, Jackie Hicks; our very talented and highly-skilled makeup artist, Latitia Thornhill; hairstylists Ed DiCamillo and Michelle

Schofield; and our graphical designer, Staci J. Cherry, we love you all for real and sincerely thank you for the impressive work on the cover photo of our book.

To our multitalented, most beautiful daughter and social media mogul Brande Elise Dora Serrano, thanks for believing in us and always encouraging us to go for it.

We acknowledge all of our family, friends, and neighbors, both near and far, for giving us the strength and encouragement to journey on.

Finally, to our publishing company, WestBow Press, and all their staff who worked on this book project, we say thank you for believing in the importance of marriage and for identifying with the concept of our story, which needed to be told in the hope that it will restore, renew, rekindle, and encourage covenant marriages to stay in the race and journey onto forever with Christ leading the way. Amen.

Foreword

Dr. Harold L. Arnold, Jr.

The global economy is built on the broad back of the corporation. These corporations, which come in all shapes and sizes, offer a wide variety of products and services to the world. The corporation is the economic engine of every industrialized nation in the world. At its apex, the corporation symbolizes unity of vision, goals, and effort. Without question, corporate success demands leadership that values mission and purpose. But, more than anything else, the most prolific corporate leaders from Paul Allen (Microsoft co-founder) to Mark Zuckerburg (Facebook Founder) achieved extraordinary results by developing products the world needs and developing the people to make these products a household commodity. These corporate masters have built systems and structures that continue to shift the innovation, productivity, and wealth of the American landscape and beyond.

Partnership conveys power. Corporate entities' power lies in the commitment of the individuals to partner in reaching business goals. But, the greatest display of partnership's power lies in the human relationship of marriage, which Christ equates to his relationship with the Church. That is a compelling comparison because Christ sacrificed everything for the Church. He asks the Church to reciprocate by sacrificing our lives for His Kingdom.

With their wealth of corporate experience and as ambassadors for marriage, co-authors Richard and Nephetina Serrano are well poised to teach us the pivotal lessons of partnership's power. Their examination of the marriage system through the lens of corporate metaphor offers a compelling perspective for several reasons: (1) nearly everyone either has direct experience with the corporation or is very familiar with its structure, (2) the multi-disciplinary nature of the corporation gives a useful framework for examining the different functions and gender role flexibility evident in great marriages, and finally (3) the corporate lens allows us to understand how differences (whether in function or personality) should be complementary and healing rather than competitive and divisive. Ultimately, the Serrano's Marriage Corporation teaches us that marriage is a multi-faceted system that depends on the commitment and strengths of the husband and wife as equal executive partners to reach its maximum potential.

Too many couples wed with an unrealistic expectation that everything is just going to fall into place because their love will conquer all. However, the Serrano's fresh framework helps us better understand that success in marriage (as in the corporation) does not happen without deliberate and thoughtful planning and execution. Couples that embrace the interactive nature of the Marriage Corporation are best poised to achieve all that God has prepared for them. In turn, God promises to reveal his deepest truths to them--truths which most couples never discover.

Just as the secular corporation continues to transform our daily lives through the systems they employ, God is asking all who believe in him to believe their Marriage Corporation holds the power to transform marriage from an obligation to an opportunity to represent Christ in every sector of the society. Even after thirty years of marriage to my wife, I continue to discover ways our Marriage Corporation can better represent the mind of Christ. Each of these discoveries takes me one step closer to being a better husband. Even more importantly, each step transforms me from a more self-centered to a more God-centered Christian. By this book's end, my prayer is that God will show you that level of personal transformation as well. I wish you tremendous blessings on the person and partner that you will become through the power of the Marriage Corporation.

Dr. Harold L. Arnold, Jr.
Author of *The Unfair Advantage: A Grace-inspired Path to Winning at Marriage, and Marriage ROCKS for Christian Couples*

Endorsements:

The Serrano's are a great gift to The Kingdom of God. Our theme has stressed Faith in Action: Families Seeking Direction in a Chaotic World. The backbone of the Family is a Strong and solid marriage. The Serrano's are part of God's Infrastructure for Strengthening Families through ministering to Marriages.

Senior Pastor, Bishop J. Louis Felton
and Lady Priscilla Felton
Mt Airy Church of God in Christ

Endorsements:

Richard and Nephetina have undoubtedly brought a fresh and unique approach to the covenant of marriage. They both bring a wealth of experience, both marital and corporate, from which they powerfully draw principles that will assist those that are married and those that seek to be married! This book is a MUST read for those that desire a deeper understanding of marriage!

Dr Gilbert Coleman, Jr.
Freedom Worldwide Covenant Ministries
Author:
Transforming the Minds of Men, Kingdom Principles for effective living, Till Death do us Part, The Unresolved Dispute there's hope for your Marriage, Straight from the Pastor's Heart

Endorsements:

I am excited about the content in this book and ready to utilize the power in the concepts it reveals. **This is a must read for everyone**. Whether you are married, getting married, or in a single head household hoping to get married, this book is for you. I have been a Pastor for 30 years and have personally counseled many couples, but I have never read anything like this book. The Holy Spirit has used Richard & Nephetina Serrano to provide the tools couples need in order to have a **great Marriage**. It presents information essential to establishing the corporate structure needed in all homes, marriages, and great families.

I have always believed that you don't get the marriage you want, you get the one you work at together. The book "The Marriage Corporation" Corporate Strategies to Fulfilling God's Purpose in a Covenant Marriage offers tremendous marriage tools and insights, using something people are familiar with, the concept of a Corporation. It is often said that America is built on the concept of the free enterprise system of Corporations but after reading this book, you too will conclude that America is built on the strength of the Corporate Marriages. God intended marriages to be a great institution and Richard & Nephetina Serrano has developed the corporate roles and structure that will impact families for generations to come.

Bishop Shawn Bartley D.D.
Senior Pastor of True United Church
CEO of True United CDC and True United Learning Center.
www.trueunitedchurch.com

Endorsements:

I have realize from my pastoral experience of over 25 years that marriage and its complicated challenges can adversely affect most Christians and non-Christians and hinder individuals and eventually the family unit. I highly recommend this book, in this book you will find several scriptural principles that will give you a basis for better marriage and family relationships. Although the enemy is interested in destroying marriages and families because this is the basis of what makes up the Church and society he cannot do so if you'll chart the course of your marriage and family relationships on the Word of God.

It is recommended to every couple who started out smoothly on the path of love and eventually stubbed their toe on something they didn't expect. This is a book for every couple. For who among us can claim to have been so lucky in love that nothing has ever jolted our relationship? Who among us is so skilled, so adept at love, that we have kept every bad thing from interfering? A number of helpful books have been written on the subject matter but none, in my opinion, deals adequately with the individual's struggle and the challenging times we live in as it have been so explicit and relevant as in this book.

The principles in this book are practical and relevant reality. The authors of this book have shown the way, their marriage of over so many years became the living model and standard for the script, as I observed the beauty and benefit of a marriage built on the foundation of the Word of God. They have lived it because if you can't live it you can't preach it to all the unmarried singles who desire to have the successful marriage the Creator originally intended. May the wisdom of this book contribute to this desire?

To all married couples whose desire it is to improve and enhance their relationship. May you apply the principles of this book to assist in fulfilling your covenant and vows and to experience the marriage the Creator originally intended for mankind?

Bishop Benjamin Amoako
Ministries
Ghana, West Africa
Grace Gospel Family Church

Endorsements:

This book is a great read. It will help the reader simplify the structure of marriage by looking at it in a way in which we function every day. Richard and Nephetina Serrano are amazing marriage counselors. The philosophy of running your marriage as a corporate entity is a strong structure that last.

They have great natural and spiritual insight that can aid the reader to a healthier and organized flow of marriage.

Marriage Corporation by Richard and Nephetina Serrano uplifts the covenant of marriage while also encouraging the submissive flow of leadership between a husband and wife.

The Serrano's are following the biblical hierarchy of a Christian household, according to the book of Ephesians chapter 5.

As Pastors and counselors, my wife and I recommend and endorse this book. We believe in their testimony and how they overcame trials and tribulation of marriage. We now see them on the other side, healed, whole and operating in God's structure. They are a great example of marriage.

Apostles Owen and Julia Ford
True Love Church
Authors:
Where He Leads I will follow, A 40 Day Devotion True of Love,
The Fight of my life

Endorsements:

The book, The Marriage Corporation, is a must read for every married couple that desires to stay together forever. It is a fresh take on marriage and comes from a very unique perspective. It will make you look at the structure of your own family and evaluate who is operating in which role. What I really appreciate about this book is the candidness from both Richard and Nephetina Serrano regarding their own highs and lows via their own union and how the concept of looking at their marriage union as a company really changed their lives. Keeping God as that third strand in your marriage and taking practical steps, such as creating policies that serve as governing tools in your household, are invaluable concepts that you need to learn more about within the scope of this book. I endorse this book for every newly married couple and even older married couples because there is something in this book for everyone. I believe this book will be on the shelves of many marriage counselors across the country because it provides practical help and divine insight from the Holy Scriptures that will explain what a "marriage corporation" actually looks like. God bless. ~ Larry and Joanna Birchett, Jr.

Apostle Dr. Larry Birchett, Jr.,
Senior Pastor of Harvest House Restoration Center
Author
'Reverence for the Storm' and 'Processed for His Purpose, Purposed for His Promise".

Prophetess Dr. Joanna Birchett,
Co-Pastor of Harvest House Restoration Center
Author
'Defeat is Not an Option' and 'Stepping Stones'.

Endorsements:

"If your marriage lacks structure, organization, and or vision you need to have The Marriage Corporation book for fulfilling God's Purpose in your marriage. Richard and Nephetina Serrano have come up with a brilliant idea to enhance unification in the marriage.

In their book you will receive a step by step guide to establishing a well organize marriage relationship that others looking in from the outside would envy. This is one book that should be in everyone's library especially if your married or planning to be."

**Rev. Kenneth and Sis. Charmian Brown,
Cofounders and CEO. Marriage Ministry Together Inc.**

Introduction

"It is not good for the man to be alone. I will make a helper suitable for him…" So the Lord God caused the man to fall into a deep sleep; and while he was sleeping, He took one of the man's ribs and closed up the place with flesh. Then the Lord God made a woman from the rib (side) he had taken out of the man, and he brought her to the man.

—Genesis 2:18, 21, 22

Whatever the size of a family unit, it needs some sort of organizational structure for it to function effectively, efficiently, and properly, the way God our creator intended. Most certainly, a marriage that suffers a lack of structure is quite likely to encounter problems, especially when an attempt to implement some sort of order is made. Put in other words, for a family to function properly, there is a compelling need for household policies.

But what is a policy? A policy is defined as a statement of intent that is implemented as a procedure or protocol. Viewed in the context of this book's subject matter, policies would be generally accepted by the members of the family after they have been developed, fine-tuned, and then adopted as procedures of protocol by the senior executive officers we call the husband and the wife, otherwise known as the president and executive vice-president of the marriage corporation.

You certainly do not want to be at risk of not operating at full efficiency and peak performance in the home. Whatever your status may be in life pastor, politician, show business celebrity, or a layperson certain crucial departments are needed for the smooth running of your household, and you simply cannot lack them, or you will surely fail. Such avoidable failure will be a sad reflection of inadequate or a total lack of proper planning on the home front. The Bible clearly states, "Without a vision, the people perish." How true this is! Well, without a plan, the people will fail. However, in the final analysis, people don't just fail. They just simply fail to plan.

You must have qualifications for specific tasks in the home. This translates to who is more qualified to perform a particular task. Let me offer an example. We all have résumés; well, at least most of us do. When we are scouting for a job, we have to offer a résumé that incorporates all the training and experiences we have had for at least seven to ten years preceding our application. The greater the experience we have garnered, the more qualified we are considered for the job in question, and naturally, we would fervently pray that there is an available opening for us. This scenario is not markedly different from what happens in our homes the only difference is that in our homes, the jobs are readily available, and all we need to do is identify the ones we are qualified for.

In our marriage corporation, Nephetina and I came into the organization with our individual home résumés, and we have strived to build them up from the period when we were in our youth, living in our parents' or grandparents' homes. So, starting from that point, we have both been able to articulate our individual experiences while growing up, and then attempted to situate them as qualifications for the different roles we are called to play in the running of our home as a marriage corporation. In other words, we have been able to clearly establish that it is what we have learned up till the present, from our differing backgrounds, that has determined what we are individually and successfully doing as partners in our marriage corporation.

Almost invariably, whenever you start on a new job, you are either trained for that position to make you proficient in it, or someone gives you a tour of the duties and an orientation on what is expected of you. Basically, this means that as you are settling down to your job, you are also getting a job description. If, on the other hand, you appear to be coming on board with more than adequate experience to see you through, then all they have to do is give you directions on specific ways in which they would like your duties performed. Either way, there will always be the need to come into an equitable agreement with your new employees on the specifics that are required from you to perform your duties with satisfactory diligence. As the Bible eloquently says, "Can two walk together except they be agreed?"(Amos 3:3).

The résumés that we have brought onboard incorporate our career summary, work history, places with dates, promotions, shifts that we worked, and emoluments that we received in the form of allowances. We have included all chores that we did and additional things that we did around the house. Naturally, we have tried to be as honest as possible in our narrative.

As I grew older, I received an allowance, and that showed me that rewards do come to all who work hard. Even in our marriages, it is important that we are rewarded in our relationship with our spouses. Sometimes, we may not easily recognize the rewards because they are not all tangible. However, even "thank you" or other simple words of encouragement can go a long way in the sincere expression of gratitude.

From the start, permit me to declare, once again, that marriage is a covenant, the terms of which will need to be renegotiated on the constant basis of the triad of compromise, concession, and common sense, in very much the same way that the members of the board of directors and the top management team of a corporate organization must work harmoniously to meet the expectations of the shareholders of the company. This means that the relationship must be constantly monitored, adjusted, and nourished. I invite you to keep eight key words in your consciousness while reading this book. These words are: maturity, communication, gratification, responsibility, compromise, appreciation, courtesy, and spirituality.

1. You must attempt a mature redefinition of what love really is.

The breathless romantic glow in which many people expect to have their emotional needs met very soon dissolves in the face of the practical realities of day-to-day living. For some, because the continued gratification of these emotional needs is an addiction of sorts, making them little more than receptacles for this sort of supportive love from the opposite sex, they sulk whenever they are denied it. But as Bishop T. D. Jakes aptly puts it, "This is dependency, not love. It is shallow, not deep. It is a mere feeling, not a commitment... a feeling that can change as moods or circumstances change... and if the feeling vanishes, even temporarily, then it is easy to decide that love has ended."

However, mature love possesses a spiritual component that has the very profound and sublime effect of converting one from a solely self-oriented person to an others-oriented person. It is at this stage that your spouse's welfare and happiness assume a greater importance than yours, since, as Norman Vincent Peale put it, "Real love is nothing more than an accurate estimate and supply of another's needs." In considering the harsher realities of our existence, another definition comes quickly to mind: real love is what results after years of surmounting difficulties together. And just as a corporation will have its harrowing moments of downturns, a marriage will necessarily be subjected to its own moments of turbulence. Clearly, these practical concepts contrast rather sharply with the romantic, starry-eyed, and sex-saturated characterization of love that is now so prevalent. But they are much closer to the truth, are they not?

The word *love* is a very active verb. This means that love is not just a pleasant feeling. Rather, it is a way of regarding someone and treating that person. The sheer activity inherent in love becomes apparent in this exchange between the late Bishop Norman Peale and a distraught young lady named Mary.

Mary: "I don't love my husband anymore."

Peale: "How do you know that?"

Mary: "I don't feel loving toward him any longer, that's why. I feel nothing."

Peale: "Love is more than a feeling. Simply commit, for the next one month, to acting as though you love him, whether you think you do or not. Do this, regardless of how you feel. The important thing is how you act, not how you feel. To act this way is not deception. It is the practical dramatization of a hoped-for image of what is to come. This is unconditional love. The really true love."

Mary's marriage was salvaged.

2. Keep the communication line constantly open.

No matter how long you have been married, you cannot afford to take your communication lines for granted. In a situation, for instance, where a couple is separated for much of the day, as most couples are, it is wise, just as we have early morning brainstorming and strategy sessions in the large corporations, to set aside a specific time, perhaps early in the morning, to talk about plans, problems, and any other aspect of their coexistence. In this way, potential difficulties can be addressed while they are still at the molecular stage. This allows the marriage to develop resistance to its attendant stress and strains. Communication assumes many tenable forms in marriage. They include: sympathetic listening, knowing when to be silent, working together, and playing together. Sometimes, it could just be a casual, affectionate touch or even a glance. One of the greatest forms of marital communication is shared laughter. Communication, in whatever form it takes, is the heartbeat of the marriage corporation.

3. Defer gratification.

Employing a combination of patience and self-discipline, both partners in the marriage corporation will sometimes need to put off or forgo certain immediate material pleasures in order to obtain greater benefits in the future. Financial stress, usually as a result of poor planning, can put avoidable stress on the corporate enterprise of a joint existence.

4. Take responsibility.

The truth is simple. It is also quite prosaic. Marriage is going to be what you and your spouse make it. No better and no worse. Face up to an incontrovertible fact: You are most unlikely to be able to change your partner very much, if at all. The only person you can really change is yourself. However, when you do effect some changes in yourself, the entire equation is altered for the better, and things begin to work out the way you would prefer. How do you change yourself? You do this by humbly accepting the blame, sometimes even when the entire fault is not yours, apologizing in a true spirit of corporate statesmanship when you should, and compromising now and then. If your partner has a habit that should be dropped, pray for him or her, rather than nag about it. Almost invariably, what your spouse needs is patience and prayers. A wise man once said: "Prayer doesn't necessarily change things for you, but it changes you for things."

5. Start to compromise.

Put in its simplest terms, compromise means that you acknowledge that there are two or more sides to every question. Learn to, in a good-humored manner, engage in some form of trade, and barter with your spouse during your coexistence. This is also what happens in the corporate world. If you will stop leaving your socks all over the house for her to pick up, she will stop attacking the toothpaste tube from the middle. If you will stop leaving your hair dryer in all and odd places, he will quit golfing on Sunday mornings and go to church with you.

6. Practice appreciation.

Psychologists are of a conviction that the strongest human need is that of approval. Everyone cherishes a word of praise. What middle cadre manager does not appreciate a note of commendation from the company president? Try to master the art of the casual compliment. Say "you look wonderful" as often as you can. An unanticipated gift for your husband. An unexpected gift for your wife. A text message saying, "I love you."

7. Practice courtesy.

Marriage should not result in the death of politeness between a man and a woman. One of the ways of showing respect to another person is by being polite to that person. Rudeness, in whatever form in marriage, must be considered an affront to any concept of civilized behavior by any right-thinking person. In fact, as the late Bishop Norman Peale puts it: "A tendency towards rudeness must be considered the mark of an inferior intellect."

8. Infuse the spiritual component into your marriage.

We cannot controvert one fact: marriage is a difficult and demanding enterprise that needs all the help it can get. What greater help could conceivably be available than that from God? Insist on keeping God at the center, and your joint troubles will be more bearable, your burdens lighter, and your joys more soul-satisfying. In every conversation between you, God should be a third person listening in. With that type of mind-set, you will be more inclined to say the right things to each other. Besides, as

God listens in on your conversations, He shares your problems, understands your needs, and watches over both of you. That way, every conversation between you and your spouse becomes a prayer in itself.

Nephetina and I welcome you to *The Marriage Corporation*

1

In the Beginning

In Genesis 1, God established an order and a structure, thereby laying down the foundation of social cohesion for all humankind with special respect to the family structure. But let us start from the beginning.Genesis 1 reads:

> In the beginning God created the heavens and the earth.
>
> The earth was without form, and void; and darkness was on the face of the deep. And the Spirit of God was hovering over the face of the waters.
>
> Then God said, "Let there be light"; and there was light.
>
> And God saw the light that it was good; and God divided the light from the darkness. God called the light Day, and the darkness He called Night. So the evening and the morning were the first day.

Then God said, "Let there be a firmament in the midst of the waters, and let it divide the waters from the waters."

Thus God made the firmament, and divided the waters which were under the firmament from the waters which were above the firmament; and it was so.

And God called the firmament Heaven. So the evening and the morning were the second day.

Then God said, "Let the waters under the heavens be gathered together into one place, and let the dry land appear"; and it was so.

And God called the dry land Earth and the gathering together of the waters He called Seas. And God saw that it was good.

Then God said, "Let the earth bring forth grass, the herb that yields seed, and the fruit tree that yields fruit according to its kind, whose seed is in itself, on the earth"; and it was so.

Seeing, with a great deal of satisfaction, that he had acquitted himself creditably with regard to the Earth's form and structure, God now focused on the habitation of the Earth. So, in Genesis 2:24, God created man and woman. Subsequently, He joined them together, declaring, "Therefore a man shall leave his father and mother and be joined to his wife, and they shall become one flesh." With this dramatic set of words, God instituted the marriage relationship. He did not stop at that. He instructed, "Multiply!"

and it became so. In total obedience, man and woman added children to their union to create the family unit. The marriage corporation was established.

A covenant marriage is intended by God to be a lifelong relationship that celebrates and exemplifies unconditional love, total reconciliation, sexual purity, and mutual growth. A covenant is an eternal commitment with God. Marriage is a vow to God, to each other, to our families, and to our community to remain steadfast to each other while purposefully growing in our covenant relationship. People can negotiate their way out of contracts, but they cannot negotiate their way out of a covenant. This is hardly surprising, for the heart of covenant marriage is "the *steadfast* love of the Lord," which comes from the very heart of God and never ceases.

After living joyously together for all twenty-eight years as man and wife, Nephetina and I are absolutely convinced that these are the nonnegotiable components of a covenant marriage:

1. Covenant marriage is the fruit of a loving and faithful relationship.
2. Covenant marriage partners must take responsibility for their actions.
3. A covenant marriage is not built on coercion, deceit, ormanipulation. A wife's submission must be freely given. It must grow from respect and not fear or manipulation. By the same token, a husband must choose to daily love his wife "as Christ loved the church." He must freely choose to love and honor her although sometimes he may not feel like loving and honoring her.

4. A successful covenant marriage is rooted in actions based on choices and not necessarily on feelings. Feelings are forever fluctuating. Therefore, to build a covenant marriage on feelings is to build it on shifting sand, which cannot support the foundation.

5. Partners in a covenant marriage must nurture their relationship. Our marriage grew as we built up each other in love. As covenant partners, we have mutually administered unconditional love, forgiveness, and reconciliation to each other while providing comfort and hope to ourselves.

6. A covenant marriage is based on freelyoffered commitment. This is because the partnership is built on selfless love that is freely given and freely received.

Let us look at creation for a minute. The first salient question is "Why did God do it that way?" Why did He create one being and then employ a part of that being to create a secondbeing who is quite clearly sexually, emotionally, and mentally different yet of his own substance? The complementariness was so valid that, on sighting her, Adam could have wonderingly proclaimed, "This is me and yet not me." And this lends perfect credence to the essence of marriage since, in real terms, the newly created Eve was Adam, his very flesh and bone. For that reason, the Bible conclusively declares, "Adam called her woman, and, for that reason a man is to leave mother and father and be united to his wife to become one flesh."

At this point, it becomes instructive to pause and examine the Trinity (Father, Son, and Holy Spirit). Since the Trinity is a family, it makes spiritually logical sense that if man was made in God's image, he also must be made a family as well. In essence, a man cannot totally comprehend the crux of his existence until he learns to exist with and for someone else. Put in other words, both relationship and communion are crucial to this process. From the teaching of the New Testament, we can see that God, in His creative magnificence, replicated the process by creating the church from the side of the second Adam, Christ, for the same reason of intimate fellowship.

The next question now becomes this: "For what reason is a man to marry a wife?" The answer is quite clear. Because woman was originally a constituent part of man, she must return to become one with him again in marriage so that the full expression and design of God's image in human beings can be revealed in beautiful totality.

Ultimately, however, within the context of this book, the concept of woman being a part of man is not exclusively tied to individuated pieces of flesh and bone. The concept is infinitely broader and certainly much more profound than that. She is the necessary complement to him that together reveals the glory of the image of God in humanity.

Her parts and his parts each have their own order and function. Together and rightly ordered, their united differences ignite the power and glory of creation itself, which is the consummate activity of God from the beginning.

By the same token, their joint existence together, as man and wife, is supposed to have a coherent order and function so that, together and harmoniously ordered, their different human competencies, skills, gifts, and natural talents can come together to create a home that gloriously edifies God's purpose in matrimony. That is the reasoning behind the conceptualization of this literary work by Nephetina and me. We are entirely convinced that God insinuated some of His mystery into the way corporations are run for monetary profit and economic accomplishment, partly for the insightful benefit of Christians to be able to draw some corollary for the smooth running of their coexistence in holy matrimony with their spouses.

2

God, Chairman of the Board

> In the beginning was the Word, and the Word
> was with God, and the Word was God.
>
> —John 1:1

His name is Jesus Christ, and He resides for eternity at the right-hand side of God. "He exerted when he raised Christ from the dead and seated him at his right hand in the heavenly realms" (Ephesians 1:20). He has a direct line of communication, and His line is never busy. "Everyone who calls on the name of the Lord will be saved" (Romans 10:13). And all who wish to call on His name only need to take particular note of any of these keywords: Jesus, Christ, Lord, Savior, comforter, and friend.

Indeed, He is Jesus Christ, the I AM THAT I AM, and is known by those who are saved as their personal Savior and Lord. He welcomes you to the entity known as the Marriage Corporation, Inc., a matrimonial organization jointly established by Nephetina and me and duly registered at the church, in the wholesome presence of the Body of Christ, some twenty-eight eventful years ago in Philadelphia, Pennsylvania. Looking solemnly at each other, we totally with our joint body, mind, and soul committed ourselves to the covenant of marriage by uttering these sacred words to each other:

> I take you for my lawful spouse, to have and to hold, from this day forward, for better, for worse, for richer, for poorer, in sickness and in health, until death do us part.

With these simple yet totally committed words, Nephetina and I declared that we saw our vows not necessarily as promises but as privileges. We were saying that we would laugh with each other and cry with each other and that we would care for each other and share with each other. We would build together and live together. We were promising to cherish andrespect each other and to comfort and encourage ourselves for all eternity. We were also promising to encourage, inspire, laugh together, and comfort each other in times of sorrow and struggle. This essentially meant we would love each other unconditionally in good times and in bad, when life seems easy and when it seems hard, and when our love is simple and when it is an effort. On that fateful day, we joined our lives together, not merely as husband and wife, but as friends, lovers, and confidants. Each person automatically became the shoulder to lean on and the rock on which to rest for the other person.

God was there. So, He knew what a special day it was for us both. For each of us, what we had previously were mere dreams and prayers for an enduring partnership, and that day was the fulfillment of those dreams. God knew all these to be the sacrosanct truth because He was present in the church on that day. How wouldn't He have been there? After all, the proceedings were conducted in His house, and He is always present in His house:

"Why were you searching for me?" he asked, "Didn't you know I had to be in my Father's house?" (Luke 2:49).

Permit me to introduce God properly within the context of The Marriage Corporation. He is the Chairman of the Board of directors of the company, and He sits not only at the head of any table within our household, but also as a silent witness to all that transpires within our home. I am pleased to declare that, for any transaction within the corporation to assume the semblance of validity, His signature must be affixed at its end. He has to be consulted before any major decision is taken within the corporation. In times of crisis, minor or major, He is always available to give His wise counsel, although I must hasten to add that He absolutely insists that a formal request to that effect is made, as He totally encourages a constant flow of communication between us and Himself. I am also happy to declare that, for the corporation to run as smoothly as it does, we, as a couple, have made it an unwavering habit to engage in constant dialogue with Him. On His part, because we do try to remain as faithful as possible, He always makes Himself readily available to direct our steps and counsel us every minute of the day, twenty-four hours of the day, seven days of the week, fifty-two weeks of the year, year in, year out. For, indeed, He is rightfully called the wonderful counselor (Isaiah 9:6). Additionally, He is the mighty God, everlasting Father, and Prince of Peace, and anyone who listens intently to Him never has a need to be afraid and will always be safe (Proverbs 1:33). God has been awesomely faithful. He makes it a point to always seek us out.Sometimes He spontaneously communicates His thoughts to us when we are in the shower, when Nephetina is cooking her characteristically delicious meals, or even while I am doing something as menial as fixing a light bulb.

Why is God totally qualified to be chairman of the board of the marriage corporation? These are the reasons. He created heaven and the earth from His own wisdom: "By wisdom the Lord laid the earth's foundations, by understanding he set the heavens in place" (Proverbs 3:19).

He also created man from the soil of the ground. Then, He breathed life into him: "I formed man from the dust of the ground. Then the Lord God formed man from the dust of the ground and breathed into his nostrils the breath of life, and the man became a living being" (Genesis 2:7). Not yet done, He fashioned out woman from a rib at the side of the man. He redeemed man from the curse of the law, and He did this so that His promise to Abraham that he would be the father of many nations would be validated in the life of humankind (Galatians 3:13,14).

Above and beyond all these, God was instrumental to the covenant arrangement between me and Nephetina. This is what I mean. A covenant marriage is intended to be a lifetime union that celebrates and epitomizes unconditional love, conjugal reconciliation, sexual purity, and mutual growth. It is an eternal commitment with God as principal witness. It was a vow to God, to each other, to our families, and to the community to remain true to each other while purposefully growing in that covenant relationship. You can negotiate your way out of a contract, but you can never negotiate your way out of a covenant. This should not come as a surprise, for the heart of covenant marriage is "the steadfast love of the Lord," which comes from God's heart and never ceases.

Jesus has remained faithful to the mission that His Father in heaven entrusted Him with, being always prompt to attend to the needs of His people, and never missing a single day of work. He is key to all the knowledge, wisdom, and understanding of God. His Word has not only been a lamp to guide us, it has also been the unfailing light on our path (Psalm 119:105). He is a total repository of all our secret thoughts, and He is the provider of all our thoughts and deeds. "Would not God have discovered it, since he knows the secrets of the heart? (Psalm 44:21).

God empowers the poor to be poor no more, heals the brokenhearted, sets the captives free, heals the sick, restores sight to the blind, and establishes in total liberty those that are bruised. "The Spirit of the Lord is on me because he has anointed me to proclaim good news to the poor. He has sent me to proclaim freedom for the prisoners and recovery of sight for the blind, to set the oppressed free; to proclaim the year of the Lord's favor" (Luke 4:18,19). Most importantly, God cleanses us of our sins: "But if we walk in the light, as he is in the light, we have fellowship with one another, and the blood of Jesus, his Son, purifies us from all sin (John 1:7–9).

The entire breadth and length of knowledge, wisdom, and understanding is with God: "For the Lord gives wisdom; from his mouth come knowledge and understanding" (Proverbs 2:6) and "in whom are hidden all the treasures of wisdom and knowledge" (Colossians 2:3). In His might, God comes to The Marriage Corporation with awesome benevolence and authority, and this is why He is Chairman of the Board. The great and mysterious truth is that we do not even need an internet connection or computer to gain access to Him. All we need do is pick up the greatest piece of literature on earth. It is called, simply, the Bible.

3

Office of the President/CEO

From when I was seven years old to the age of nineteen, I lived in my parents' house in Philadelphia, Pennsylvania. Basically, my career as an active participant in the smooth running of our home started from when I was seven, and at that age, being so small, all that was required of me was to help with simple chores around the house. Between the ages of seven and ten, I generally helped with making the beds, neatly setting up the table at dinner, and putting away the clothes in the appropriate closets and wardrobes. When I turned ten, I started sweeping the floors, dusting the furniture, washing the cars, and washing small portions of the walls. Our walls tended to get very dirty, largely because a lot of the time, when we came down the steps, we would literally come flying down the staircase with our hands gripping the wall for support, and so, naturally, the walls could get horribly smeared with our soiled hands. It was also at about the age of ten that I started going to the store at the street corner to do transactions on behalf of the family. Like most families in the neighborhood, we had credit at the store, and I would be asked to go and make purchases. By the age of thirteen, I started getting allowances of between five and ten dollars for my work in the house. These allowances came in very handy because we needed money for the movies and the usual candy and popcorn purchases. We were no different from the other children in the neighborhood. The only difference, I suppose, between my family and some of the other families was that our friends, who also shared our need for money, would take money from their parents. Our parents were well aware of this and certainly did not want us to fall into that bad habit, and so they ended up killing two birds with one stone by ensuring that we were well funded but had to earn the money. This achieved the twin objectives of steering us away from juvenile petty crime and instilling the core values of gainful industry in us.

Our parents pretty much kept us on our toes, as it was common for us to hold down two to three jobs during the week and even more at the weekends. In fact, for me, the weekends could get quite busy. As I grew older, I would join my father in cutting the grass and cleaning the yard. We would sweep the yard and then thoroughly water it for dust control. For this particular job, my father used to pay me from his own pocket. I still recall, not without some amusement, how my mother would continually peer out the window to make sure that the yard was spick and span. She was that fastidious. After that, I would clean not only the front of our house, but also that of our neighbors to the left and to the right. My mother insisted on this. Her thinking was that we could not quite consider the front of our house clean if our neighbors' were not also clean. She actually considered their grounds an extension of ours. And this had absolutely nothing to do with whether the neighbors took any notice of or even remotely appreciated our heroic efforts to keep their environment clean on their behalf. In retrospect, I believe that there was every likelihood that the neighbors actually thought their children were doing the cleaning, but we knew better. Frankly, it was more than likely that anytime their children came out, ostensibly to clean their surroundings, and found it clean, they simply went back inside, totally relieved that their job had been done for them. Interestingly, I still do the same thing here in my own house. Anytime I clean the back of our house, sweeping and watering, I extend my efforts to the back of my neighbor's house, and I'm sure he is usually quite happy that someone has relieved him of that burden.

Back in those days, we also used to apply soap, bleach, and hot water to the front steps of our house. As I grew older, I came into the fascinated realization that, although we were a Catholic family, my parents still subscribed to the old Spanish superstition that to ward off evil spirits, one had to thoroughly clean the front steps with bleach and hot water. Interestingly, the members of the Spanish community in North Philadelphia still engage in that practice to this day.

By this time, I was also cleaning the walls of the house more actively and vacuuming the rugs. I also kept the dinner table in perfect order, mopped the floors, and changed the curtains with the regularity that my mother demanded. My mother was very particular about the seasonal changes in the interior decor of our house. She had winter curtains, spring curtains, andsummer curtains, and as each season arrived, we would have to bring down the curtains of a previous season and put up the new ones for the new season. There was always so much work to do, and my mother kept us on our toes all the time. She had all the time in the world to do this, because while my father went out to work to fend for the family, my mother stayed back to keep and preserve the home front running in perfect order. So, for all practical purposes, she was the foreman of the house, and she supervised us with the discipline of a regimental sergeant. If we lacked any tool to work with, she would waste no time in getting it for us. This is why my mother must take the greater part of the credit for how I have turned out to be the handyman around the house that I am today.

My father had certain tasks that were particular to him and him alone. I recall that we had a twenty-two-gallon fish tank that was elaborate in its possession of accessories to the last detail. It had its own motor and its own backdrop and other fittings. While we were growing up, because of the intricate nature of the fish tank, my father would not allow anyone to clean it, except himself. However, as we grew older, my brothers and I gradually assumed the responsibility of cleaning the fish tank as well. In 1979, at the ripe age of sixteen, my father began to teach me how to drive. Most of the work my father did at the construction company where he worked involved driving tractors. Tractors were driven to flatten the concrete at building sites. Actually, my father was working at a construction and landscaping company. Ever since I knew my father as being in paid employment, this was the only place where he worked. So, at fifteen going on sixteen, during the summer months, my father would co-opt us to go and work with him at the company, where he taught us how to drive the tractors. At this stage, I did less and less chores at home, because during the week, we were fully occupied working at the company. The company paid us for the work we did during the weekdays, but my father paid us out of his own pocket on the weekends. The tractors were of different types. I recall that I drove the tractors that leveled concrete and dug holes in the ground. I also learned to drive bulldozers. A lot of the jobs included the construction of tennis courts and swimming pools, and I assisted my father with these jobs mainly over the weekends. Sometimes, I worked at drilling very deep holes in the ground. It was a lot of hard work, and one could safely call it hard labor. But it was very fulfilling, especially since we were now earning wages in a formal setting.

We were also taught to contribute to the finances of running the home, and a certain percentage of our paychecks went toward a common pool of monetary contribution to the smooth running of our household. My mother was quite particular about good quality furniture for the house, and because of this, I recall that we had a high turnover of furnishings at our home. The transactions were all based on a very credible credit base. These days, you would go to the furniture store and purchase your goods using your credit card. But back in those days, the furniture salesmen would actually deliver to your house, and we had a system. We usually bought on credit. Each month end, the salesmen would come to our house with their books. I gradually grew into the role of the person handling such transactions. The salesmen would record my initials in the books as having made the payment for the month. This was our duty as young adults. It was very significant for us because we learned how to transact business at this early age. My mother trusted us implicitly to make these due payments, and we never abused her trust. In fact, much earlier than this, I had already started handling such credit transactions at the corner store. I recall running back and forth between the store and the house, getting the bill, and then going back to make the payment. So, my mother pretty much prepared us for a life of integrity in business transactions, and I have definitely carried over all that knowledge to the running of my own home. In many respects, my siblings and I were very fortunate to have the kind of industrious and visionary parents that we had.

Naturally, not all homes in the neighborhood were as well organized and disciplined as ours, and at that stage none of us realized how unique our home training was. It wasn't until I had gotten married and had to start managing my own home that the essence of all that my parents had instilled in us hit me with the force of insightful realization. We did not do much cooking, that being strictly my mother's department. However, we did assist in the kitchen, sometimes with prepping, and then washing the dishes. Even now, although Nephetina is the main cook, I still help with very minor prepping, simple recipes, and washing the dishes. The Serrano household was one that was organized to the finest detail of contributory performance by all the members of the company. My parents worked their corporation with clockwork efficiency. They were running the Serrano house, and they did not compromise on their standards in doing so. We, the children, were the workers. We were the crew. They would put up the work list for the week on Sunday. We had a list for hours of operation, midshift, and after-school hours. The chores were listed for Monday through to Sunday. On weekdays, we had one or two daily chores, while on the weekends, we had two to three chores. If, however, you worked outside the home, which began to happen when my brothers and I approached our midteen years, the weekend chores became less. Although even this respite could not be fully guaranteed most of the time, my parents tried their best to honor their word.

Each marriage corporation will obviously come with its own attributes. For instance, in the process of structuring your marriage corporation, it is of paramount importance to know who is a day person and who is a night person. In addition to the time of day being an important factor, some people tend to work better alone, as opposed to working with another family member. It also salutary to note that if you are not getting enough sleep, that can play a big role in the mood swings that one can easily experience. I recall that when I was young, I worked all shifts and in every department of the house. In fact, it was not uncommon for my mother to wake us up in the middle of the night to make amends if we did not clean the dishes to her rather exacting standards, and there was usually no room for negotiation in this regard as my mother believed that you do not put off until tomorrow what you can do today. With her, it was simply a question of "no questions asked," but when you knew the rules and polices of the home and abided by them, all went well. Let's be honest about one thing. Even now, we want to experience the thrilling feeling of being appreciated every bit as much as we lapped up praise when we were much younger. My parents truly appreciated us for helping them to give life to the order and structure they had fashioned for our home. It was also clear that they appreciated our total and obedient sacrifice in maintaining and sustaining the integrity of their marriage corporation. I am able to deploy a lot of hands-on skill in my own home today because of the tremendous experience I gained from working under the marriage corporation of the Serranos. Structure, imagination, and creative originality were all in place. I have largely adopted a lot of what I learned from my parents' home in my own home today. Indeed, cleaning and maintaining the house is such a big part of everyday living for us, and I am more than qualified for most of the jobs that I am applying myself to in my home.

Reflections

1. Great leaders are not always seen but are always felt.
2. You can be fired by God in your own home and not even know it, because you have lost your authority through neglecting your responsibilities.
3. It is easy to build a house, but more difficult to build a home.
4. See your wife's complaint as a problem requiring a solution.

— 4 —

Office of Executive Vice President

In an interesting manner, I am an only child. Yet, in real terms, I am not. I say it this way because I am the only child from the union of my biological father and mother. However, I am still part of a larger family of two other children from my father and another three from my mother.

My very early years were spent growing up in the daily care of my maternal grandmother at the four-bedroom house in West Philadelphia where we lived. My father and mother went their separate ways when I was eleven months of age, and largely because my mother had me at the rather tender age of seventeen, the responsibility of providing motherly care for me fell on her own mother, with whom I became quite close. My grandmother took care of my daily needs, which included preparing my breakfast and sending me off to school. She passed on when I was twelve years old. Because of the separation of my biological parents at an early age, I did not relate to any appreciable degree with my biological father, and the lot fell on my stepfather to raise me when we lived in a four-bedroom house in West Philadelphia.

I recall quite easily that my grandmother was a very domesticated woman, and because we were quite close, I had the opportunity to adoringly observe her at fairly close quarters as she went about her household chores. She was pretty much a homemaker. We lived on a block that had families with several children, probably averaging about five to each family. In fact, my own mother was one of six children. I grew up in the knowledge that my grandmother was an excellent cook. However, I will have to quickly admit that, while I can't remember watching her cook a lot of the time she was in the kitchen, I certainly recall relishing and enjoying the delicious dishes she placed before me.

My grandmother was also quite good at keeping a neat and orderly home environment, and my earliest memories are of a home that was without the usual clutter you would find in most homes. Every part of the house was kept in perfect order, and you might safely say that everything had its place, and there was a place for everything.

Another woman who influenced me tremendously in my early years was my mother's elder sister. She was a very good cook. When you combine her cooking skills with that of my grandmother, what you had was, for me, a life in which I had nothing short of the most delicious meals. And, between them, they did a lot of cooking.

My mother's younger sister, under whose influence I also came, spent considerable time doing my hair and generally keeping me looking like a little doll. Because of this, I tended to view her more as an elder sister than an aunt. Apart from her, those early years saw me living in a house of four boys. They were my cousins, my younger brother, and an uncle who was my grandmother's youngest child, and it wasn't until I was seven years old that we had a female addition to the family.

My mother was also a very good cook. When I was around eleven months old, she began to date my stepfather. He was a very industrious man and provided quite well for our family. In fact, even while in college in Indiana, he kept a job as a deputy sheriff. But, because he lived far away, we witnessed a lot of the absences of my mother, as she traveled back and forth between Philadelphia and Indiana to spend time with my stepfather, by which time they already had a son between them.

Later, however, at completion of college, my stepfather relocated back to Philadelphia, and we all began living together as a family. At this point in time, my mother's cooking skills became more obvious. She cooked everyday, and she cooked very well. So, from this background, the source and origin of my own cooking skills become only too obvious.

My own cooking career started on a somewhat dramatic note when I was nine years old. At this stage, let me emphasize that, while ours was not exactly a wealthy home, I never got the impression that we were poor, and I pretty much got all I desired as a little girl. I recall wonderful birthdays whenI received beautiful presents and everything else a young girl could possibly wish for. But my mother suddenly started going to work. She worked the hours of 11:00 p.m. to 7:00 a.m. as a night auditor at some hotels in the Philadelphia area. That meant she was absent from home on most nights. I soon easily and naturally slipped into the role of cooking for the family and very soon became an expert of sorts in frying chicken, cooking corn, and steaming vegetables. In addition to this, my younger siblings were pretty much babies at this time, and I became a nighttime babysitter. My younger brother and I attended school across town, and I became responsible for our safe daily passage to school and back on the local bus. My little sister was a baby, so while my mother was away at work, it became my responsibility to feed her and change her diapers at night.

Between the ages of ten and fifteen, I often moved between my aunt's house and my mother's house. However, at the age of eleven, I went to stay with my aunt, my mother's elder sister. She was a wonderful person who ran a well-structured and well-ordered home that I simply grew to love. She did not require me to do much cooking, perhaps because she herself enjoyed cooking so much. But she did train me on some other household chores like keeping my room tidy and cleaning the furniture. Her house had a sizable porch where she liked to keep nice outdoor furniture, and she loved to keep that space very tidy and beautiful, and I enjoyed helping her out with that. She also had two beautiful front gardens, and she loved spending time planting and maintaining them while nurturing the plants and flowers.

My aunt was a bit of a dreamer. It was from her that I learned the enjoyable pastime of going out on bus and car rides just for the recreational fun of it. She would often on weekends drive my cousins and I to the more affluent suburbs of Philadelphia and New Jersey, and we would admire the big and beautiful homes with their elegant driveways and expansive grounds. In later years, I would continue with this pastime and would often just take buses on joyrides around the districts of Philadelphia and New Jersey.

My aunt took me on my first visit to Penn's Landing, the beautiful, serene, and tranquil Philadelphia waterfront of the Delaware River. To this day, this waterfront paradise remains one of my most favorite spots for spending time alone with my Lord, my husband, and myself. I would often go there with my journals and notebooks and spend hours on end praying, meditating, and simply thinking through the issues of my life in one of the most tranquil environments I know. Penn's Landing has lost quite a bit of the serenity it offered in those days, because it is not as secluded as it used to be.

At the age of thirteen, I went back to live with my mother and stepfather at their home in South Philadelphia. The environment was a bit different from my grandmother's home in West Philadelphia, where families on the block tended to relate rather closely. In South Philadelphia, the children mainly just related with one another. My parent's home was very comfortable. I had a room to myself. It was the largest room in the house, and I shared it with my adorable little sister, while my brother had the middle room and our parents had the front bedroom. We had designated chores around the house. My dad pretty much delegated the responsibilities, and I had a specific designation to do the dishes, while my brother and I alternated the cleaning of the only bathroom in the house. In between these, we had joint responsibilities for cleaning our room walls and keeping the floors sweptand carpets vacuumed.I started receiving an allowance at this point, and it became quite fulfilling to know that I was earning my keep as a part of the family.

My movements between the homes of my grandmother, aunt and mother can best be explained by the dysfunctionality of my growing-up years. My early childhood was not quite as tranquil and well-ordered as my husband's. This was probably why my maternal grandfather, now a bishop, decided to take a more than passing interest in my development. From the age of twelve, he became a very strong influence in my life, especially the spiritual aspect of it. He would come over and take me out on rides around town, during which he regaled me with stories, or to one of the many Christian fellowships that he frequented. He also loved visiting people in their homes, and he took me everywhere with him. My grandfather, through this well-orchestrated early and active exposure to Christianity, was largely instrumental to the development of my close relationship with God, and I accepted Jesus as my Lord and Savior at the age of twelve. His influence on my spiritual life was undeniable. I believe that he could sense that I was now ready to develop a special relationship with God, and so he decided to be the person that would lead me to God, and I must say he did a very good job of it.

So, basically all I have narrated so far is supposed to give you a broad picture of the attitudes and skills that I have brought into my marriage, as a way of presenting my own résumé. I have found the running of our home very interesting and fulfilling indeed. I am very fortunate to be married to a wonderful man who was raised by very disciplined parents to be responsible and industrious. He is very much a hands-on sort of man, which has made the orderly organization of our home rather efficient. We generally handle most of our household chores by ourselves, but allow me to say that if both the husband and wife do not have the required qualifications for a particular task, they will have to outsource the work to an outside contractor.

The résumés that are brought to the home should also include any additional training, such as in communication skills. How well do you communicate with and understand each other? How developed are your people skills? Do you practice your love language? Have you had formal training in accounting methods? Do you know how to negotiate? Are you capable of appropriate self-control when it is demanded? Can you work independently and without supervision?

It may yet turn out that some responsibilities in the home are being done by default by someone who said they are qualified for the position but actually did not live up to the expectation. It is sincerely recommended that members of the corporation be totally honest with each other and declare in their résumé only what they know to be true and honest, as the Bible says quite clearly, "A house divided cannot stand."

Reflections

1. Your early years are nurturing years.
2. Early family life can be early training years. Treasure them.
3. The language of love is the most effective communication tool.

5

The Spiritual Hierarchy

Everyday begins and ends with God. That has become a nonnegotiable component of my life with Richard. Without fail, I awaken from sleep with a single statement on my lips: "Good morning, Jesus!" Almost invariably also, I could have a song that I'm humming in my heart as I slip out of bed. However, the main plank of my quick internal devotion at this time of day is to sincerely express a word of gratitude to God for according me the privilege of witnessing the dawn of another day. Fully aware that some people went to bed the previous night but did not wake up, I am filled with gratitude for what I consider a special gift of another day in which I can glorify the essence of my existence by putting in a good day's work, marveling at the sheer awesomeness of God, and the opportunity to minister to His people.

Interestingly though, most of my encounters with God are in the shower. I have grown into the habit of having my little conversations with God while I'm taking my shower. I also deliberately steal moments in the shower just to enter into conversation with Him. The process goes on while I'm dressing to go to work. And, incredibly enough, most of the direct revelations I have had from God have come to me in the shower. It is actually incredible. It is

The Spiritual Hierarchy

almost as if God accepted that the shower presents a favorite place for me to commune with Him, and He in turn started to visit me more often while I'm in the shower. It is interesting that some of the best ideas I have had for books have occurred to me in the bathroom. Even some beautiful songs that I have composed were given to me by the Holy Spirit in the shower. Even remarkable words of inspiration and ministration to despairing couples during our covenant ministry have come to me while having my bath.

Another very important prayer venue for me in our home is our prayer room. Over the past twelve to fifteen years, Richard and I have been blessed with the capacity to have a dedicated prayer room in wherever we call home. This prayer room has come to occupy a very significant part of our prayer life. I tend to do a lot in there. I pray. I meditate. I study. Sometimes, I just sit quietly and engage in very deliberate breathing, just listening for and to God. So, basically, we spend our designated prayer time in this prayer room. However, I will have to admit that, because I am constantly in motion while I'm at home, my designated prayer times are often sporadic, as I could simply decide to go into prayer even during some domestic activity. I consider our prayer room a truly blessed place. I'm beginning to think that when you consciously dedicate a space in your house to God, that space gradually starts to acquire its own special aura. It becomes a house of God, so to speak. This is because anytime I go into our prayer room to devote some quiet moments to God, the insights that I receive and the tranquility that I experience can only be described as amazing.

My workplace is another important prayer venue for me. While I'm at work, I constantly take moments during my break time to pray and talk to God. But there is no doubt that my greatest moments with God are in the shower. We have three bathrooms in our home, and sometimes, I just stroll into any of them to steal a few moments with God. Sometimes, I forget myself in there and my husband has to shout out to ask if everything is alright. Some of the most amazing assignments that God has given me came while in the shower, and quite a few of them are still being fulfilled to this day. The major difference between my communication times in the shower and in the prayer room is that while I'm in the shower, God speaks to me, and while I'm in the prayer room, I speak to Him.

In conclusion, for me, it is communication with God throughout the day. However, at the end of the day, my husband and I try to put in a half hour of devotion before retiring for the night.

Nephetina and I are very fortunate to work at the same organization. Like she said, even our workplace is not exempt from our consistent prayer life. Usually, our first break time at work is between nine and nine fifteen in the morning. We have made it a habit to meet at the conference room at work and have a quick joint prayer. Sometimes it may be that I had earlier received a communication from God and want to share it with Nephetina, and this break time provides a wonderful opportunity to conveniently do so while the news is still hot.

We tend to have more intense prayer times together during the weekends. On Saturday mornings, we spend a lot of time together in the prayer room, while on Sunday, we jointly devote time to God before church and then after church. But, as she mentioned earlier, we have grown into the habit of viewing the entire day as an opportunity to commune with God. For instance, even at work, we try to have lunch together as often as possible, and while this is not usually a prayer time, it is an opportunity to share quality time together and discuss any pending issues, especially with regard to our couples' ministry. At any one time, we usually have an average of five couples we are counseling. So, if our phone schedules at work are not too tight, we squeeze in time to schedule appointments to see the couples for counseling or even say quick prayers for them on the phone. Therefore, even at work, we are continually praying for both ourselves and the couples we are ministering to.

Actually, we have had some simply amazing experiences in our prayer room. I easily recall one Saturday morning. We were due to speak at a church out of town later that day, and it was obvious that we needed some form of intense preparation for that day's activities. Nephetina had arrived at the prayer room before I did. When I came in, I found her on her knees in a corner of the room, and she was deep in a prophetic prayer. I could feel the presence of the Holy Spirit. For a moment, I stood rooted to the spot and simply marveled at the awesome power of spirit. When I joined her, our devotion seemed to ascend to another level. It was incredible. I will never forget the intensity of that singular session. As the power of the Holy Spirit descended upon us, we prayed that day would be one of massive soul-winning for Christ and that God would use both of us to deliver His people from the shackles of sin, such that the awesomeness of God would be revealed in their lives. That prayer room, in that hour, became a dense repository of the magnificent power of the Holy Spirit; therefore, what transpired later in the day did notcome as a surprise. This is because our speaking engagement had sucha powerful response that we could not believe that God could use us so much in the course of His wonderful work. Later that morning, still in the prayer room, we anointed each other. First, I anointed Nephetina on her forehead, eyes, mouth, ears, heart, hands, and feet. She, in turn, anointed me in all those parts of my body. We did this joint anointing so that our assignment for later that day would be blessed in all we saw, touched, and heard and so that our hearts would be clean and steadfast in the delivery of God's message.

Now, the concept of joint and mutual anointing is one that we accord some seriousness to in our marriage. It not only guarantees that, through it, we reaffirm our joint covenant with God, the chairman of our corporation, but that we also appoint ourselves as ministers for each other. It is instructive that, while discussing with our friend, Dr. Yomi Garnett, he observed that the singular act of anointing ourselves, in itself not being a common practice among couples, is indication that Nephetina and I are married not only for our own sake, but also to set a veritable example for what couples should do to glorify the essence of God in their lives and in their homes, and that was why He gave us the peculiar ministry of covenant marriages to oversee.

Nephetina and I have been anointing each other for years. In fact, we started anointing each other when we bought our first house in the third year of our marriage. As I recall, it was just something that God gave Nephetina, and since she initiated it, we have never looked back on that activity. What I have discovered on the personal level is that it makes me feel good and safe. It's almost as if Jesus Himself came down to bless me, and the fact that it's my wife who is doing it on His behalf only allows me to recognize her immense importance in my life. In our ministry, we usually encourage couples to anoint each other. Sometimes, we come across a couple who is always bickering at each other, and we ask each of them to anoint the other person's side of the bed. At other times, we come across a couple who are having a serious spiritual conflict in their home, and we advise them to anoint their house all over.

Our prayers for each other are also, of course, very important. Nephetina prays that God continues to give me the requisite wisdom to continue to lead our home in spirit and in truth, in accordance with the will of God. On my own part, I always pray for her. If for instance I was going to leave her at home and go somewhere, I would not step out of the house without saying a word of prayer for her, and vice versa.

For us, our prayer life has been a tremendous journey all its own. I believe that I can unequivocally declare on behalf of the both of us that the fundamental bedrock of the successful marriage corporation is an equally successful prayer life. To God, our chairman, be all the glory. Amen.

Reflections

1. Always pray together.
2. Always pray for each other.
3. Always anoint each other.
4. Your prayer room is your power room.
5. Your quiet time with God is your strongest time with yourself. "In quietness and in confidence shall be your strength…" (Isaiah 30:15).
6. A successful married life depends on a successful prayer life.

— 6 —

The Department of Planning and Strategy, the Chief Accountant, the Legal Department (Contracts, Negotiations)

And my God will meet all your needs according
to his glorious riches in Christ Jesus.

—Philippians 4:19 (NIV)

I am the chief accountant in our home, and I can tell you straightaway that it is a heavy responsibility. When you operate joint accounts, and you have two people spending money at the same time, you discover that you now must engage in a very delicate balancing act. This becomes even more challenging when you are not necessarily making so much that you can go to bed with both eyes closed. My wife and I share everything. Even our personal bank accounts are shared. It is really in the realm of finances that God's prescription that the two shall become one manifests itself totally. The bedrock of absolute trust and unity truly shows itself in how well a couple can harmonize their spending in such a way that their home can be as comfortable as they sincerely wish. For the convenience of expenditure, we have a dedicated joint account for the payment of bills. However, as I've already pointed out, the biggest challenge comes when enough money is not necessarily entering that account in such a way that you can have peace of mind and can purchase enough to keep the home in the comfort you are accustomed to. For us, careful budgeting has become a rather crucial activity. Thankfully, Nephetina always has the presence of mind to keep me abreast of our needs. She usually tells me when we are running out of certain vital items in the house. This is important because, at some point, I'm usually preoccupied with writing checks for house rent, electricity, and other things. What you find is that incoming paychecks may not necessarily balance up to outgoing checks, and that is why careful budgeting becomes very important. So, at some point, we must pause and ensure that we have sufficient funds to stock up the house for the next couple of weeks. The accounts department controls the flow of money within the home. It also determines the things we can do in ministry and in other parts of our lives together. Take our date nights for instance. Spending time together is a very important part of any marriage agenda, and Nephetina and I have continued to have date nights on Fridays, despite our increasingly busy ministry schedule. We still catch a movie together or go to a favorite restaurant to eat. On Saturdays, since we enjoy the outdoors, we would go to a park. However, these days, we tend to spend a lot of time at home instead, simply enjoying each other's company. The advantage to this slight adjustment in our lifestyle is that we end up saving money. This brings home the truth that you do not have to spend money to enjoy yourself. Let's face it, one of the most beautiful and profitable dividends of a covenant marriage is that you can enjoy yourself in the company of another person without having to spend a dime! These days, we have grown into looking forward to spending Friday nights at home just enjoying each other's company. Look at it this way. This is the beauty of a covenant marriage. The marriage is already a "park" by itself. Because it is providing all the pleasantness of a bright, sunny day, the park is already in the marriage, so you can visit your marriage at will as if you are visiting a park. You can have your picnic in the park for the simple reason that the marriage itself is already a picnic.

Periodically, I call a meeting of the accounts department as the head of that department. Usually, these are at times when certain pressures for spending out of our usual pattern emerge. For instance, God may have instructed that we do certain things in ministry that require spending money. So, Nephetina and I would have an emergency board meeting to sort out details of how to meet such obligations. Naturally, we experience no anxiety at such times because God, who gave us the assignment in the first place, would be present at the head of the table as the chairman of the board. We would juggle the figures. We would see what bills cannot wait and those that can wait. We would decide on what to do without in the immediacy and what remained crucial, no matter the situation. Ideally, such meetings should involve the entire household, including the children. Apart from the children learning from an early age how to engage in budgetary expenditure, it is also good for all parts of the corporate entity to contribute to the budget exercise. Children must be clear about what they can and can't have and why they can't immediately have it. They can then grow up with a sense of financial propriety and a strong sense of money discipline. It is quite possible that one of the reasons for the great deficit in proper monetary values in society today is a result of insufficient involvement of the children of a marriage in the budgeting and expenditure of their home in such a manner that they arrive at a fine appreciation of the true value of the money that their parents work so hard for and spend on their needs.

Basically, this how Nephetina and I operate. We have a dedicated joint account from which we pay our bills. The funding of this joint account is from our working paychecks. We pay in 90 percent each of our income into the account. Nephetina pays her tithe into a separate account, while I pay my tithe from the joint account. After this, we then pay our bills from the account. Also, we always have it at the back of our minds that we are still individuals with our own unique needs. When we need private items like clothing, our spending also comes from the joint account. Special occasions demand special dispensations. So, for instance, if it were my birthday, then by joint agreement, it is accepted that I can draw on the account to buy myself some things as a birthday treat. At certain other times, Nephetina, for instance, might have a need for some items of clothing. She would inform me, and I would glance at our account balance and then approve a spending budget for her. This is one of my roles as the head of accounts. We pretty much go out shopping together, and we ensure that we get true value for our money. We tend to visit shops where we know we can get quality items for fair prices. Admittedly, we cannot avoid expensive items sometimes, but we do try to get bargain prices most of the time. The bottom line is that we try to stick to our budget.

We are only too human. Sometimes, we just see things that catch our attention, and we would like to acquire them. It is sometimes difficult to keep that acquisitive impulse in check. What have we done to contain that impulse? Simple. We cut up our credit cards many years ago. We do not have credit cards. Nephetina and I haven't used credit cards in fifteen years. Every couple will have their own experience, but we learned some harsh lessons much earlier in our marriage. We had credit cards that we simply were not mature enough to handle with a high sense of propriety. When we did not have sufficient money, we fell back on our credit cards as crutches to see us through. The result of this was that we were living above our means, most of the time spending our incomes even before they came in. The truth is that if you don't have enough, you simply don't have enough, and that is that. We decided to get used to that fact, refusing to spend money that we did not have, at least in practical terms. You see, Nephetina and I read a very good book called *Financial Planning*. It was written by a gentleman named David Ramsey. A statement he made in the book struck a chord in me. He said, "Keep it simple, stupid!" He went further to ask a rhetorical question. If you went into a store, and you saw something you liked but did not really need, and you had a credit card in your pocket, would you buy it? For most people, the obvious response is yes. Now, if you went into a store, and you saw something you liked and did not really need, and you had cash in your pocket, would you buy it? For most people, the answer is no. So, Nephetina and I reviewed our answers, and when we were convinced that we were shortchanging ourselves, I collected her credit cards from her. I cut up all our credit cards. It was difficult parting with those cards. We were quite unhappy for sometime, but we eventually got used to no longer carrying them around. Nephetina had some cards she truly cherished. She had Macy's, JCPenney, American Express, and a host of others. Even today, she feels a pang of pain at offers of 20 percent discounts at Macy's for cardholders. But we simply had to get rid of those cards, and we are happier with that decision today. We spend less, and in a more disciplined manner, too.

Another decision we have taken to protect our finances is where we bank. We discovered that some banks charge you for not having a specified balance in your account, and such balances can be quite high. We are not too comfortable with that. We work hard for our money and see no reason why we should be penalized for not having a specified balance. So, we bank more with the credit unions these days. The credit unions offer better rates, and their minimum balances are very low or nonexistent. Apart from that, they are more familyoriented and more willing to grant you a loan should you need one.

Have we had any drawbacks from not using credit cards? The only glaring drawback is that we cannot do much online shopping. Naturally, there are many advantages to online shopping. It saves time. With just a couple of clicks of your mouse, you can purchase your shopping orders and then move on to other important things, which can save you a whole lot time. Another advantage of shopping online is that there is no need for vehicles, which means you do not burn fuel. This saves you money. For some people, online shopping will save them energy because it can be tiresome to shop from one location to another. Thankfully, for Nephetina and I, this is not really an issue, as over the years, we have pretty much identified specific storesfor specific needs. There is also the advantage that you can compare prices before buying items online because of the advanced innovation of search engine. Additionally, online shopping stores are open twenty-four hours of the day, seven days a week, and 365 days a year. It is very rare to find any conventional retail stores that are open in this manner. The availability of online stores gives you the freedom to shop at your own pace and convenience. Looking at these advantages, it is quite possible that Nephetina and I may, at some point in the future, think very seriously about doing some of our shopping online. Hopefully, at that time, we would have gained sufficient maturity to handle credit cards with the matured dexterity that they call for.

Reflections

1. If you can sleep together, you can bank together.
2. The two shall become one, and their accounts shall become so too.
3. You don't have to go to a park for a picnic. Your marriage is already a picnic.
4. Have a budget not only for running the house, but for each other's needs.
5. Have regular expenditure meetings.
6. Credit union banking is wise banking.
7. Minimize your load of credit cards.

7

The Maintenance Department
(Shopping, Stocking the Shelves)

Whatever your hands find to do, do it with all might.

—Ecclesiastes 9:10

The maintenance department is a twenty-four-hour department. It is a continuous process. I head the maintenance department. There are so many things to think about all the time. I generally provide technical assistance to the members of the household.

Generally, however, I receive written or oral orders on every aspect of the running of the household. The list is endless. Broadly, this important department involves general cleaning of the house and the carrying out of minor maintenance duties as they rear their heads. Fundamentally, to keep track of the state of the house, periodic and constant general inspection is needed to ensure that everything is in place and that nothing is needed in certain areas. A key part of what I do is make sure that maintenance equipment is always in working order. For instance, only a couple of days ago, my wife informed me that one of the bags in a vacuum cleaner was full. At such times, I act immediately. I keep spare bags in the garage, and so I went down immediately and replaced it. This, of course, shows that the maintenance department is a twenty-four-hour, seven-days-a-week service, and the work is never finished. Naturally, for the smooth running of this round-the-clock sort of activity, it is essential to have a stock of supplies of spare parts of equipment, and I always ensure that this is the case. As I go round to ensure that all is in perfect working order, I also plan for the next day, taking note of certain items that might require attention.

I am very particular about the rugs. Many people suffer from allergies, and my wife and I are not exempt. Besides, we keep a cat as pet, and his hair is exposed to the rugs. So, I make it a point to vacuum the rugs in the front room, stairway leading to the bedrooms, and the stairway leading to the basement. I try to do this twice a week; once during the week and then on the weekend.

Initially, I did not realize that the maintenance department was as vast and time-consuming as I now find it. I actually thought it was more about taking care of the exterior of the house, mowing lawns, and replacing dead security lights. Now I know very different. The maintenance department actually runs the entire house, since all the equipment provides the technical backup for the smooth running of all we do. In fact, it was a real awareness of the existence of a maintenance department that brought about the concept of this book in the first place. I still recall the day. I was in the basement, idly tinkering with my tools. Nephetina was on her way up the staircase, when she suddenly turned around to inform me that a light bulb needed changing. And, surprisingly, I simply told her to put a ticket in! I really don't know why I said that on the spur of that moment, except to conclude, of course, that God had a message for me. In the corporate setting, if anything goes wrong, you would be required to put in a ticket, which is like a note detailing a fault and its location. Such information is fed into the computer, and all the maintenance crew has to do is generate the information from the computer and get their work done. The only difference in the home is that we are face to face with each other and can therefore communicate directly. Nephetina knows who I am. But, in the corporate setting, you don't get to know who the maintenance crew is. So, when I told Nephetina to put a ticket in, or even better, send me a text message so that I can start keeping a record of maintenance work in the house, I glanced up, and at that moment, God told me that this was the maintenance department, and it ran the entire house efficiently. At that surreal moment, I looked at my tool board on the wall. I looked at my three rows of tools and three rows of drawers containing hammers, nails, screws, tapes, and all such other mechanical items, and I had an experience of total discovery in which I humbly told God, "Wow, You are right. This indeed is the maintenance department, and it runs the whole house!" That was how the book you now hold in your hands was birthed.

Now, at this point, it becomes very important to highlight what can sometimes become a sore point in a marital relationship. Almost always, you have a situation in which a wife is constantly reminding her husband of things that need fixing around the house. There is always something that needs to be repaired; the refrigerator needs to be moved to a particular spot, the sink is getting blocked, or the bathroom needs tissue paper. Sometimes, these constant reminders can frankly begin to seem like nagging. Yet, the issues exist, and they need to be resolved. What I discovered in my own experience was that I immediately arrived at the conscious awareness that my role as the general fixer of mechanical issues around the house was a department that had a name to it, and I lost all sense of frustration at such constant reminders. My awareness of the existence of a maintenance department in which I was in charge gave me a certain sense of responsibility that I could no longer deny. If the bulb died, that wouldn't be my fault. But if the dead bulb was not replaced, that would be my fault, since it is my duty to ensure that it is replaced, and I would be found wanting in the discharge of my responsibility if I failed to replace it. That is the beauty of being aware of your department in the house and reconciling yourself to that fact.

In some homes, where the maintenance department is concerned, there could be a role reversal. This is what I mean. Generally, men are traditionally in charge of the mechanical aspects of the smooth running of the home. However, I have seen instances in which the woman appears to be more inclined to mowing the lawn, changing the light bulbs, and doing all such traditionally male activities. Almost invariably, you will discover that it is because they grew up that way and have become quite competent with technical household chores. As I mentioned at the beginning of this book, each partner comes to the home with certain credentials on their résumé, and it is important to appropriately identify each person's strengths and weaknesses so that they can run the house efficiently. Therefore, when a man comes into conscious awareness of the fact that that the maintenance department is his own territory, two things happen simultaneously. First, he no longer feels a sense of frustrated inadequacy anytime his wife reminds him that he needs to change a light bulb because he knows full well that she is merely reminding him of his duty. Secondly, since he now knows only too well that maintenance is his forte, he is more inclined to attend to repairs and supplies even before she notices such needs around the house, thereby preempting her need to remind him. The result is a better harmony in the way they run their household, and they can better appreciate the cooperative component of their matrimonial union.

Put differently, God has given you the gifts of what you can competently handle around your house. He is the chairman of your marriage corporation. To remind you of your responsibilities, he tells your wife instead to relate that message. If you listen to her in a levelheaded manner, you are listening to God. The situation is not very different in a corporate setting. Management has set a certain job description for you. When you slack in these responsibilities, you are given a verbal notice. The more notices you get, the more obvious it becomes that you are lacking a sense of responsibility. In your home, your wife is not your boss, but she represents God, the chairman of the board, in communicating with you. Ultimately, the more easily you do what is needed in a timely fashion, the more you create the enabling environment for a peaceful and harmonious relationship between you and your wife.

It is also important to realize that a core motivation in being in charge of the maintenance department is to assist the wife, children, and members of the household to lead a decent domestic life. In the corporate setting, the workers in a building will always notify the company's maintenance department if they notice a fault somewhere. The same thing applies to the home. All the members of the household should adopt the responsibility of drawing the attention of the maintenance department to current faults in the house, and the maintenance man should be able to take such information in good faith. His eyes cannot be everywhere at the same time, and he needs the cooperation of the wife and children to keep him informed of issues that need to be attended to as they arise.

The grooming of the exterior of the house is as important as that of the inside. Lawns, in particular, are very important. In my own case, I contract out the mowing of our lawn. This is because I have allergy problems that could be awakened by exposure to grass. Either way, it is important to ensure that the lawns are immaculately groomed. I tend to clean the outside of the house at least twice a week. The day before and the day after trash collection are very crucial days, as I've discovered. The day before, a lot of trash accumulates, and the squirrels and racoons are all over the place rummaging among the garbage. Besides, some trash from the neighbors can add to ours to make quite a load. Then, after trash collection, the trash trucks tend to spill quite a bit of garbage on the ground. This is why I find it necessary to clean up at least twice a week. I clean up the back of the house thoroughly and hose the sides of the house, including that of the immediate neighbors. This is a carryover habit from my parents, who believed that the exterior of your house is not clean if your neighbor's exterior is dirty. Another aspect of cleaning is the shoveling of snow during the winter. I keep at least three shovels in the house. Snow can build up pretty fast. It takes me at least three hours of shoveling to clear our immediate surroundings of snow so that we can easily exit the house when we need to. It is also especially important to shovel around the cars so that they can move. Once the snow recedes, there is usually a residue of salt on the cars, which can sometimes take an hour to clean.

Communication is very important, and because of this, a system needs to be in place. Not everyone has a good memory. That is why a system for communicating household needs is important. Sometimes, short notes to the maintenance department or reminders of what needs to be done can work. Other times, phone or text messages can be equally useful. Nephetina and I have a system in which we tack short notes on the refrigerator reminding ourselves on what needs to be done. This can be quite helpful amid a hectic work schedule. She reminds me of things that need to be fixed, while I remind her of certain items that appear to be running out of stock, especially groceries.

Additionally, it is my job as the maintenance officer to make sure that my wife has all she needs for the smooth running of her kitchen department, and that includes cooking equipment like blenders, magic bullet, deep fryer, vegetable chopper, and the George Foreman grill. Suffice it to say the same thing goes for my department. I have to make sure that household cleaning items are available at all times. These include mops, brooms, dusters, and vacuum cleaners for cleaning hallways, windows, and rugs. My wife actually joins me on some minor aspects of maintenance work. For instance, she helps with dusting of furniture and mirrors, and she also does some sweeping anytime there is a need for it. Carpentry, electrical work, plumbing, and general repairs fall within my sphere of responsibility. Occasionally, there is a need to touch up on some painting somewhere in the house. I generally do this, but if Nephetina can spare the time, she joins me. Once in a while, I invite a neighbor to join me, and they usually oblige if they have the time. Naturally, I reciprocate the gesture when I am needed. So, one doesn't have to do it all alone. Sometimes, you could become so overwhelmed with other responsibilities that it becomes really heavy, and there is nothing wrong with engaging a technical person for a fee.

The disposal of trash and garbage is also of paramount importance. We tend to accumulate a lot of reusable items like cans and bottles. My wife joins me in getting all such items down to the garage periodically, and then I gather them all together and take them outside in time for trash collection days by the city authorities. The replenishing of supplies is another core function of the maintenance department. There are many such items, including paper towels, toilet paper, soaps, lotions, and toothpaste for the bathrooms. Between my wife and I, there is no hard and fast rule about who picks up what. Whoever it is convenient for usually picks them up as the need arises, so we pretty much complement each other's efforts here. Another important aspect of my job is proper coordination for our events. Normally, when we have birthday parties to which we have invited guests, I would get out the approximately required number of chairs and tables from the garage. It is always important to know exactly what you have in store and what you will need.

Safety should always occupy a prominent place in the mind of the maintenance officer running the department. Take our house, for instance. We don't have a lot of electrical outlets. So, what I have done is to procure remote control switches that control sets of lights and appliances. This saves us the trouble of walking all over the place flipping on switches. All we need do is flip on one switch, and a set of lights automatically comes on. I also try to make sure that I avoid clutter for our safety. I don't allow stuff to accumulate, pretty much believing that everything should have its own place and that there should be a place for everything. It makes for better organization of my thoughts, and I can generally function much better as a human being.

In conclusion, the aim of the maintenance department is to consistently seek ways in which everyday living in the home can be made easier. For instance, the day my wife rolled her eyes and agonized over having to walk long distances was the day I decided to install remote switches for different sets of lights and appliances in our home. Interestingly, virtually any aspect of everyday existence in our homes can be made much easier. All it takes is going over to your local hardware store orthe Home Depot and telling them what your challenge is and asking them how to make it easier.They will avail you not only with the appropriate advice, but also the tool to make it easier!

I conclude this chapter by asking you to identify what shift you actually do in the maintenance department, as this will make you more organized. It is true that maintenance of the home is a twenty-four-hour job. It never stops. However, there will be that segment of the day that you can seriously devote to caring for your home. In my own case, I leave home for work at five o'clock in the morning and get back home in the late afternoon. That means, where my home's maintenance department is concerned, I do the second shift. And I do it with all pleasure and to the glory of God.

Reflections

1. A well-maintained house is a well-run home.
2. The maintenance of a house is a twenty-four-hour duty.
3. In telling you what needs fixing around the house, your wife is relating God's instructions. Listen.
4. Proper maintenance makes everyday living easier.
5. Avoid clutter for safer living.
6. The exterior of your house is not clean if your neighbor's exterior is dirty.

8

The Cybertech Department
(Social Media, Computer, Internet)

Let the words of my mouth and the meditation
of my heart be acceptable in Your sight, O
Lord, my strength and my Redeemer.

—Psalm 19:14

Cybertechnology, as mainly represented by the social media platforms of Facebook, Twitter, Instagram, and others of their ilk, has rapidly evolved into one of the most powerful forces in the world today. They can be beneficial, educative, and enjoyable, but only if they are used in a way that honors God. Sadly, we all know there is a lot that happens online that does not honor God, with some of them even being done in His name. In our ministry, Nephetina and I are critically aware of the enormous responsibility that is attendant to proper use of technology, and each day we ask for wisdom to deploy its use only to the glory of the Word of God and the sanctification of the saints.

Because of the nature of our ministry, the cybertechnology aspect of our lives is one of the most significant. Actually, we are both in charge of this department, if only because we have equally important and mutually supportive roles to play in it. By nature, I'm not the sort of guy who can multitask. I long ago discovered that I'm more comfortable handling one task at a time. Take our website, for instance. I am in charge of updating it constantly. Recently, I have been preoccupied with updating and uploading our promotional pictures and images, our advertorial flyers, and certain important information about our ministry. More significantly, I have also linked our website to the website of the bookstore where people can purchase the book that you now hold in your hands. This has entailed adding some text about the book to the website information. Nephetina and I have had to strike some form of compromise here. Initially, she felt that the words were perhaps too many. However, I felt that people deserved to know a bit more about the book than simply being told it's an awesome book! The truth is that a lot of people will be talking about the book, but they also need to get relevant information about it from the book's authors. We have, however, been able to arrive at an equitable compromise on the amount of information we will allow on the site. So, basically, what this means is that we mustagree as to the contents of the website, including but not limited to the volume of words. Take the music score on the site, for example. We both listened critically to the music and concluded that it's presence on the webpages merely served as a distraction from the important messages on them. So now the music only plays on the homepage of the website. Ultimately, we have decided on a broader website that encompasses all that we do, so I'm working with the website designers to create a one-stop destination that will tell the complete story of our work and our ministry.

Flyers constitute a very important component of our promotional package. We work on these flyers together. Of course, we outsource the production of the flyers, but this is only after Nephetina and I have arrived at a concept that suitably captures the message we are trying to convey. Even at the production stage, Nephetina and I must give the final approval for the concept, text, and images for the flyer.

Our consultant on this book project, Dr. Yomi Garnett, once raised the observation that we seem to place a lot of emphasis on images, pictures, and videos. He even went as far as saying that we appear to deploy a lot of attention to our physical appearance, especially with regard to our dress sense. He was absolutely right. However, our motivation goes much farther than appearances. A lot of the images we generate on our covenant marriages website and on our Facebook pages are meant to serve the specific purpose of depicting us as an everyday couple who invest a lot of effort and time in their marriage. Visuals mean a lot in communicating messages. Our intention is to encourage couples to spend more and quality time together, and we try to achieve this objective by posting images and videos that show us together at different forums. In addition to this, we make every effort to ensure a consistency in all we post on social media. This is what I mean. If we post, say, an image of us at a unique church event on Facebook, then you can rest assured that is the same image we will post on Instagram and on Twitter. The essence of this is to make sure that those who are more focused on a particular social media platform will never miss our posts. We try to exemplify what we counsel couples to do by living true to our teachings and then capturing the scenes of our life in images on social media. We also try to be as consistent as possible in all these. Sometimes, we focus more on text messages, especially scriptures. Our consistency in the sort of material we post tends to ensure that our audience knows what to expect from us at any given time. When we attend events, we deploy a lot of energy to capturing images of us together. We do the same thing on our date nights. The ultimate objective is to teach other couples that marriage entails a lot of work. What this translates to is that even if you both have your full-time jobs, a fulfilling marriage still demands that you create quality time to spend in each other's company. This is actually working at your marriage.

We have also created a rather unique way of ensuring that people who do not get to attend our events still benefit from them. This is what we do. Whenever we have an event, or a speaking engagement in the form of a seminar, or an empowerment session, we record it and put it on our website. This is because of our discovery that, while quite a number of people may not be inclined toward attending our events for any of a number of valid reasons, they are usually happy to listen to the recording while driving to work or watching YouTube during their lunch hour. In the final analysis, I think we have come to appreciate the importance of technology in our ministry, with special emphasis on social media. That is one of the reasons why we are completely overhauling our website to make it much more innovative and responsive to the needs of our growing audience. The influence of media is becoming more and more evident with each passing day. We have had young people walk over to us and saying, "Hey, my parents need to listen to you!" or "Can I have your call cards? I know someone who needs to listen to you!" That is one incredible trend we have noticed. Very rarely does anyone ask for our call card without collecting an extra card for someone else. Indeed, we have discovered that the possibilities with social media are not only incredible, but limitless. Because of this, I would say we are on a continuous learning curve.

We try to learn through hands-on experience, but also through reading and experimenting with new applications.

I tend to be very selective about what I post, and because of this, it does take me some time before I do my postings. I always insist on posting what I believe is the right material for posting. Social media is truly powerful, and it is both a force for incredible good and for veritable bad. I have found social media such a pervasive influence that the mere fact that a person follows my posts can attract some other people to become my followers. This is one reason why I am very particular about protecting the integrity of our image and our ministry by insisting that people receive from us only what is truly worthy.

The world of social media is, to a large extent, one of make believe. We realize that people tend to develop perceptions on social media that may often be at odds with stark reality. We are also aware that virtually all the images we post on social media cast us in cheerful and enthusiastic light. Truly, there is a conflict that we believe needs to be resolved since, unlike the ideal image that social media tends to portray of people, life is not exactly always a bed of roses. Fortunately for us, God has also given us the grace of our various speaking engagements as an opportunity to share stories of our own personal struggles with our audience and how God continues to give us the strength and the fortitude to endure our private and public pains. However, in letting people know that we inevitably pass through our own deep, dark nights and very cloudy days, we realize also that we have been appropriately positioned to be seen as beacons of light in a long, dark tunnel. Because of this, we are always quick to point out that when the going gets tough, as itsometimes will, the tough have to get going. We teach constantly, both on social media and at our speaking engagements, that the strongest weapon against adversity that people posses is prayer. We let people know that prayer allows their spirit to be lifted in that dark situation. As the psalmist says in Psalm 40, verse 2, "He lifted me out of the slimy pit, out of the mud and mire; he set my feet on a rock and gave me a firm place to stand." Prayer allows you to tell God that you are facing very big challenges, and because you are in communion with Him, prayer affords God the opportunity to tell you that He is bigger than those challenges you are facing. So, it's all about how you overcome, rather than how you succumb. We let people know that they cannot do anything by themselves. It's only the Holy Spirit that can see them through their challenges, as God tells them that they must stop seeing their situation through their own eyes and rather see their situation through His eyes. When we realized that people tend to listen when we speak to them, Richard and I started to ask God for more and bigger speaking engagement opportunities and even greater windows through social media for us to pass our message of hope to wider audiences. We realize now that we do have a voice, and that we need to get across to people with that voice.

The truth is, through our one-on-one sessions and the social media, Richard and I do have a lot to share with people. We have a need to let them know that we did not just arrive at this point of stability in our lives. We have been through a lot of the pain that countless people out there are going through. We have had our periods of terrible insecurity. We know what it means to be dispossessed of our home and have to sleep on the cold, hard floor. We know what it feels like to lose two cars in one day. We know what it feels like to be homeless. So, these and many other past agonies are the sort of realities we want to share with our audience, so that they can come into the knowledge that with God, all things are possible.

This is the kind of opportunity that the media accords us, and we sincerely cherish it.

Our vast exposure to the effects of social media has taught us that we must stay humble and focused. I was reading the other day that women tend to desire very strongly what they see as the ideal. A lot of singles may see us, and viewing us as role models, wish they could be like us. This is likely more of a problem with women than with men. Yet, they may not actually be ready for marriage yet. So, we really must continue to see our work in proper perspective and remain focused, humble, and free of distraction. In all we do, we try to be as real as possible.

Nephetina's mother, for instance, is sometimes surprised that we do not engage in pretensions in her presence about expressing our real feelings to each other. We try to be as nice as possible to each other at all times, but let's face it, we do have our own episodes of interpersonal tension. And, quite frankly, the mildly irritating way we would mutually address each other in the privacy of our home is pretty much how we would do so in the presence of family members. So, we try to keep ourselves as real as possible at all times. Yet, we also realize that we must, at the same time, continue to maintain an ideal of discipline, love, and respect in a world in which a lot of people have a total misconception of how a true Christian marriage should be. Some couples actually believe that it is perfectly normal to have terrible rows, sometimes leading to domestic violence. We even hear of some women who find it abnormal if their husbands don't hit them every once in a while.

We should all remain who we truly are. We should not try to be anyone else. That way, we remain true to ourselves and true to those who are close to us, because everyone else is taken. As I already mentioned, I maintain our website. But as far as its content is concerned, we both agree on what should go on it and what shouldn't. Then, as far as social media is concerned, Nephetina does most of the actual posting, while I am more focused on the presentation, in terms of flyers and images. This is principally because Nephetina is much better than I when it comes to putting material together and posting it. I do all the formatting of what we intend to post, and Nephetina goes through them to make sure it's all in order. Take colors, for instance. I am color blind. So, Nephetina sometimes has to reconfigure the color combination to make sure that it comes out perfectly, and of course she proofreads the text also.

Communication is of paramount importance. We have each other's passwords to all our social media outlets.This is purely a reflection of how open we are with each other on social media. Although we have our joint public profile pages, we also have our private accounts on social media, and we have each other's passwords to these accounts. The left hand knows exactly what the right hand is doing on social media, as it were. Essentially, this means that a couple's involvement with social media should be an open book.

In the immediate future, we want to concentrate a bit more on videos, with special emphasis on YouTube. You can't post on YouTube with phones. This must be done using the computer. So, I'm right now in the process of getting a camera so that we can have a lot of our material on YouTube. I intend to download the camera in the computer, open a YouTube account, upload it, and then interface it with our website.This is important because, while a lot of people might not necessarily be on Facebook, Instagram, or Twitter, they often visit YouTube and can now be exposed to our work.

I am generally in charge of our computer hardware. I make sure that our systems are constantly updated and upgraded, cleaning them out and ensuring that the internet is always functioning for our daily use. I try to make sure that we have optimal internet speed, but of course, we will always want it to be as fast as possible.

One thing that is getting clearer and clearer to us is that social media offers so many possibilities and capabilities that we haven't even explored yet. Because of this, we are basically still researching how we can get the best out of social media. In fact, we deliberately study audience reaction and response to specific posts and try to see why some posts seem to be more popular than others. For example, people seem to respond more enthusiastically to our vacation posts. We don't really know why this is so. Perhaps it has to do with something about us on vacation stirring up latentemotions in people. We do not know for sure, but it is a trend we have taken note of. We are using social media to take people back to the basics. We are using social media to preach that families should eat dinner together and that couples should pray for each other both at home and before leaving the home. We are not just posting a picture of ourselves on a date night for the sheer fun of it. We are posting it to drive home the message that a couple needs to spend quality time together to continue to nurture their marriage. And overall consistency is very important to us while doing all these. We try to ensure that all our social media outlets receive all we post for the benefit of our audience. I only recently became familiar with HootSuite, which allows one to post the same material on all the social media platforms at the same time. Instagram is about the only platform that offers this facility, so HootSuite is obviously very useful.

There is an appropriate protocol for the use of social media. One of the tragic consequences of the boom in the use of smartphones is that people have abandoned crucial human contact for technology. These days, even at the dinner table, most people are still engaged on social media. We think there should be a place for everything. People have been known to put their jobs in serious jeopardy just because they cannot tear themselves away from Facebook while at work. Husbands and wives have been known to be on their phones as the last activity before sleeping. Social media should not be allowed to come between a couple, and the smartphone should definitely not be the last thing we look at just before bedtime. The dinner table ought to be an enjoyable family forum, not a place where family members are competing to see who is more active on social media.

In our opinion, cyber technology is so important that people and organizations ought to have some form of formal training in it. The truth is that most people are largely ignorant of the workings of technology and only pick up bits and pieces of rudimentary knowledge with time. But, especially in ministry or in running a business, it is probably better to invest in proper and formal training so that one can have a very sound footing in technology. Nephetina and I actually engaged a professional to train us on different aspects of social media and internet usage. As it happened, we were preparing for an important event, and we wanted to link our PayPal account to the Eventbrite account for those who wished to register and pay for attending the event. So, we had this lady come over. She gave us a very rewarding three-hour tutorial on most aspects of internet use, including social media. She even taught us the best times to post on Facebook for maximal audience reception. All in all, the investment has been worth every dollar that we spent on it.

In conclusion, the children of a home should be incorporated into the cyber tech department as much as possible. Children tend to be quite savvy about technology and can help to drive a very effective social media campaign. So, they should be involved, as it also helps to monitor their own use of social media.

God knows about social media. He permitted its existence. Therefore, all reasonable attempts should be made to deploy social media for the benefit of His work and His kingdom.

Reflections

1. Let your image on social media be your image in real life.
2. Know each other's social media passwords. The left hand should know what the right hand is doing.
3. Facebook is good, but your marriage is better. Do not allow social media to come before your intimacy.
4. Engage a professional to train you on different aspects of social media and internet usage.

— 9 —

The Culinary Department
(Cooking, the Kitchen)

I give you every seed-bearing plant on the face
of the whole earth and every tree that has fruit
with seed in it. They will be yours for food.

—Genesis 1:29 (NIV)

I am in charge of this department. That should hardly come as a surprise. To the best of my knowledge, from the beginning of time, wives have usually taken charge in the kitchen. This has always been the traditional view of the domestic setting. The wife sees to the dietary needs of her husband and children. However, the point should be noted that this traditional norm is undergoing rapid changes in many societies all over the world as more and more men are developing skills in an area that used to belong exclusively to women. Also, please note that this book is about who is generally best qualified to do what is necessary to effectively run the marriage corporation. I have no doubt in my mind that in certain homes, the husband will be the better and perhaps more enthusiastic cook. Should that be the case, a role reversal ought not to come as a shock to us, as what is important is that the best person for the job does it, especially when it is also done with passion. In my case, however, I have always loved cooking. I started cooking when I was only nine years old. I had early exposure to the kitchen through my mother and her sisters, all of whom happened to be excellent cooks. In fact, at a point, I literally took over the kitchen and cooked for the entire family when I was growing up. When Richard and I started dating, one of the first things I did was learn how to cook Spanish dishes. Even in those early days of our relationship, it was obvious to me that I would be in charge of the kitchen, and I certainly wanted to be able to satisfy my future husband's accustomed culinary tastes, even though I was also well aware that I would experiment a lot with different cuisines during our marriage. I recall that what fortunately happened was that we had a Spanish neighbor who took a lot of interest in me. She started teaching me how to cook Spanish meals. She helped awaken my creativity when it came to cooking. Indeed, I became really creative with my cooking. For instance, instead of cooking just spaghetti and meatballs, I would add chicken and hotdogs. It was all so interesting. For me, the challenge went far beyond an eagerness to please Richard, especially since he also turned out to be someone who was perfectly willing to try foods he hadn't grown up with. I was also thrilled to learn how to cook foreign dishes, being someone who is always willing to learn new things. I think this sort of attitude is very important for the smooth running of the culinary department of a home. One must be willing to be innovative to make that part of the home a delight. I oversee the kitchen, and I sincerely commit myself to making sure that I am qualified to occupy that position. Take my mastery of Spanish dishes, for instance. The Spanish do have a lot of interesting recipes that can turn cooking into a chef's absolute delight. I was very fortunate to have also come under the influence of my sister-in-law. She taught me how to cook so many wonderful Spanish dishes, especially the traditional ones. One of my most favorite is the dish called Spanish Black Rice. It is a rice dish made with octopus and squid. That dish is absolutely divine, and Richard loves it too. So, generally, I am pretty much open to learning to make my kitchen experience one that will bring pleasure to my home.

Right from the early days of our marriage, we have always done our shopping together. We gradually slipped into a pattern that suited us perfectly. Almost invariably, we would shop for all our major food items in such a way that stock would last us about two weeks, and we only dropped into the shops for general supplies like eggs and milk. Our major shopping for groceries takes place at Sam's Club in Philadelphia. The great thing about Sam's Club is that it is one of the few big food wholesalers in the United States. In fact, their major customers are the numerous food retailers, corner shops, and restaurants that abound everywhere in the United States. The advantage for us is that, because this is a wholesale sales point, prices are of the best bargains one can get anywhere. We get the best possible prices for all our grocery needs, which we purchase in bulk to last us at least two weeks. Richard and I totally enjoy shopping at Sam's Club together. Usually, Richard gets one of their enormous shopping carts and follows close behind me as I carefully make my choices of the various items we need. I take my time in making these crucial choices. While it is true that, over time, I have become quite familiar with the exact items that I want, I still make it a point to carefully select, based on pricing and preferences. Another important thing that I painstakingly do is study the nutritional components of all that I select. Not only am I concerned with ensuring that our various accustomed meals give us a nutritionally balanced diet, I also want to make sure that we eat in a healthy manner. As we are advancing in age, it has become imperative that we eat not only for nourishment, but also for optimal good health. We make our shopping a truly wonderful experience.

For me, cooking is a very elaborate art that has a process. To start with, I prefer to have all the ingredients that I need to cook a meal all arranged on the kitchen table before I even start cooking. In my personal experience, failure to be organized in this fashion can easily result in a lot of frustration and even alter the outcome of a meal negatively. Richard and I have grown into a system whereby he is available to lend a helping hand with prepping the ingredients that I need for cooking. Almost always, these are the vegetables. He preps them for me so that the whole process becomes much easier. Again, after the meal, he lovingly clears the kitchen counters and does the dishes.

In the early years of our marriage, Richard loved to make breakfast for us, especially on Saturday mornings. He was particularly good at making pancakes. Other breakfast dishes he was good at included Cream of Wheat, which is a kind of porridge. He also enjoyed making oatmeal, eggs sunny side up, and toast. In fact, for Richard, this was the ultimate on a Saturday morning. Pancakes were a particular specialty of his. However, as time went on, when it became obvious that I was spectacularly skilled in cooking, and Richard came to enjoy my meals more and more, he finally left all the cooking to me. Although I sometimes miss those delicious pancakes he used to make, I truly enjoy cooking for him. For me, cooking for my husband is not a chore. It is simply something that I take tremendous delight in doing.

My cooking pattern is not complicated. I usually cook big and elaborate breakfasts only on the weekends. During the weekdays, our breakfast is quite simple. We alternate between boiled eggs and oatmeal during the week along with yogurt and fruit. For lunch, we tend to be a bit versatile. Almost invariably, our lunch would be a dinner leftover, or we might purchase lunch. Richard is fond of leftovers, while I tend to prefer fresh meals, like a salad or tuna or a soup. Saturdays are when I really do my heavy cooking. I cook three different types of meals, and then I package them to store away in the refrigerator. I try to put as much variety as I can into my cooking. For instance, I could make spaghetti with vegetables and either fish or chicken. Another typical dish for me is mashed potatoes, fish, and vegetables. Sometimes, I do a sautéed vegetable dish. We tend to take it a bit easy with starchy foods these days. I concentrate more on protein and vegetable dishes. It could be sautéed spinach and mushrooms, or chicken, or even baked salmon. Another favorite Spanish dish of mine is sardines cooked in tomato sauce with onions and peppers. This is traditionally served with white rice. However, it can be served with brown rice or jasmine rice. Richard loves the left overs from this particular dish. By preparing my meals on Saturday, it allows me to do other chores throughout the week. At one time, Richard loved peanut butter and jelly sandwiches, and I would package this for him as a snack as he left home for the day. During the winter months, I enjoy making big pots of soup, stew, and pot roast and storing them in the refrigerator. There was a time when beef stew was a favorite for us, but now we take beef stew occasionally, as we have drastically reduced our beef intake.

In my opinion, one should cook for the home in such a way that people enjoy eating. That is why cooking three different types of food and storing them in the refrigerator can be so convenient. It allows for the satisfaction of differing tastes and palates. I know that in some homes, some parents have a problem with cooking separately for the kids. However, engaging in some variety while cooking can easily take care of this. But, ultimately, what is of paramount importance is that the meals are nutritionally balanced.

Reflections

1. Gain knowledge of your spouse's culture to cook your way into your spouse's heart.
2. Be willing to be innovative to make your cooking a delight on its own, so that your kitchen experience can be one that will bring pleasure to your home.
3. Shop for food together, as part of spending quality time together.
4. Establish a cooking pattern that will make your kitchen adventure a thrilling and convenient one.
5. See cooking for your spouse as not necessarily a chore, but as something that you take tremendous delight in doing.
6. Buy your groceries at wholesalers where you can get the best bargain options.
7. Cook your meals with nutritional balancing in mind.

— 10 —

The Chief Security Officer

My people will live in peaceful dwelling places, in
secure homes, in undisturbed places of rest.

—Isaiah 32:18

The job of the home's chief security officer is a twenty-four-hour,
seven-days-a-week, year-round service. I must confess that it is
the most critical of my duties as the president of our marriage
corporation. But this should not come as a surprise. After all, as
the president of the corporation, a husband is uniquely equipped to
protect the family. However, there is more to protecting the family
than simply being the physically stronger partner in the union and
taking the proverbial bullet in place of one's wife and children.

I am responsible for the physical security of the family. God has
not only given men greater physical strength than women but has
also given men the need and desire to be their protectors. It is the
responsibility of the man as CEO to use this God-given strength
to protect his wife and ensure that she feels secure at all times. It
is of paramount importance that the wife knows that her husband
will protect her even at the cost of his own life. The husband must
be the first to cross the line into battle. Ultimately, this is because

he knows that "greater love has no one than this, that someone lay down his life for his friends" (John 15:13). And what greater friend does a man have than his wife? Besides, does a man not love himself sufficiently to protect himself at all times? Well, since that is the case, he must also extend the same level of protection to his wife, because "in the same way husbands should love their wives as their own bodies. He who loves his wife loves himself" (Ephesians 5:28).

Let's assume that during the course of the night, there was a sound downstairs, and there is every possibility that it's a burglar. Would you say to your wife, "Honey, you know this is a very fair union between us. I went downstairs the last time. Now, it's your turn to go and check out the noise"? Even if your wife had a black belt in karate and could finish off the burglar with just one good kick to the solar plexus, you had better be ready to hand in your resignation as president of the marriage corporation the next day so that she can become the CEO in your stead! The husband is to love his wife as Christ loves the church. "For the husband is the head of the wife even as Christ is the head of the church, his body, and is himself its Savior" (Ephesians 5:23). Christ loves the church to the ultimate extent of laying down His life for it. He considered His life nothing in comparison with the task God had appointed to Him. As a godly ordained husband, a man is obliged to imitate Jesus Christ in this.

Most especially in our country, burglary has become a serious threat to security and even life. The FBI recently reported that over 2.1 million burglaries took place in the United States in 2012. That this figure translates to one burglary every fifteen seconds merely goes to underscore the alarming fact that it is incredibly easy for burglars to gain illicit entry into other people's homes. As the chief security officer, what I can safely say is that my principal aim in all I do is to secure our home to prevent the casual burglar from gaining entry. Admittedly, it is practically impossible to make the home 100 percent secure, but there are certainly measures that I take that assure me that at least 90 percent of the job is done at all times.

The first thing is to adopt the security of the home as a consistent habit in which every member of the household agrees to take part. Essentially, this means that a routine should be adopted that incorporates very simple rules, such as: making it a habit to lock every door and every window when leaving the house, after entering the house, and before retiring to bed at night; refusing to open the door to unwelcome visitors and uninvited persons; and closing and locking the garage door at all times and activating the alarm system at all times, even during very short trips out of the home, like a quick visit to the corner shop.

In our home, Nephetina and I have our separate keys to the house. It is very important to identify those who can be in possession of the main house keys, since this will allow you to monitor restricted access into your house. In cases where a main house key serves many members of the household, one very common feature is the hiding of the key under a doormat or inside the mailbox. But, as has been proven time without number, most experienced burglars are only too aware of this domestic arrangement and very easily let themselves into many homes. More innovative strategies must be devised. Also, car and house keys should not be placed near the door or left exposed inside the home. Such security items ought to be kept hidden in a designated cabinet or drawer.

Another very integral part of the home security is exterior lighting. I have made sure that I installed outdoor lighting near each point of entry into our house. Also, I am always on the lookout for any burned-out lightbulbs, and I replace them immediately. I have discovered that locks are the weakest point on any door. Therefore, I have ensured that the locks on our doors are very strong deadbolt ones that penetrate the doorframe. And I always make sure that I inspect all doors to eliminate any weakness in them. The garage door is locked at all times. I also make sure that I check the windows all the time to make sure that their locks are properly in place.

Reflections

1. Securing your home is a critical twenty-four-hour, seven-days-a-week, and year-round assignment.
2. The head of the home provides both spiritual and physical security for the home.
3. The security of the home is a crucial activity in which every member of the household should take part.

— 11 —

The Benefits Package
(Investment, Returns, Insurance,
Profit Sharing, Respect)

Husbands, love your wives, just as Christ loved
the church and gave himself up for her.

—Ephesians 5:25

At the beginning of one's working adventure at a corporate organization, one of the first things that happens is that the human resources person hands you a document called the employee handbook, which spells out the conditions of service. Apart from the details of your job description, this document (usually in the form of a small booklet) also gives details of the benefits package to which you are entitled. However, even before this, you would have received an offer letter to which you would normally respond, accepting the offer of appointment. In fact, it is only after you have accepted the offer that you would get the benefits package. Likewise in marriage, in the first instance, you are being asked to accept Jesus Christ into your life. In other words, God is offering you salvation through marriage, and the only way you can access these benefits is through Jesus Christ. In any case, you do not really have a marriage corporation until you are married in Christ. The employee handbook you are given comes in the form of the Bible. This is because the Bible is the instructional manual that contains the full complement of directives that will guide you along the delicate terrain of marriage. Naturally, this instruction manual details the reasons why God created man and woman in the first place and then goes further to instruct on His policies and prescribed procedures concerning the institution of marriage. Put differently, the human resources person, in the form of the pastor, hands you the instruction manual, in the form of the Bible, which will guide you in the marriage corporation and detail the benefits that will accrue to you during the course of your marriage.

One of the significant objectives that Nephetina and I sincerely hope to achieve with the concept of benefits as explained in this book is that perhaps premarital counseling, as we now know it, should go a step further. Rather than merely focusing on what makes singles ready for the institution of marriage, they should also go into the details of what benefits a couple can expect from a marriage founded on God's commands and instructions concerning the institution of marriage. This theory is validated by the fact that no other institution in the affairs of humankind, when truthfully and conscientiously embarked upon, brings as much joy in the form of benefits. Another component that can add divine flavor to premarital counseling is to highlight the glaring differences between the increasingly popular institution of cohabitation. This is totally at a variance with God's prescription for the joint existence of a man and a woman under the same roof and the true institution of marriage. The point must be stressed that no benefits whatsoever accrue to a couple living together because the Bible, the instruction manual, does not in any way recognize it as an institution bound by the rules of a covenant. This is true in much the same way that you cannot just stroll into a Walmart superstore and start arranging shelves like any other employee. That cannot happen because you have not been formally employed to do so and the management does not recognize you as an employee. The greater tragedy of cohabitation is that the Bible specifically warns against fornication. This means not only are there no covenant benefits to be derived from it, it is also a reproach in the life of its partakers.

Right from when you are employed at a corporate organization, you become familiar with the statutory provisions of the 401(k) retirement plan clause, which states that the company will match whatever percentage funds you put in and pay you cumulatively at retirement. So, if you put in 50 percent, at retirement the company will match your 50 percent, and you get paid 100 percentcumulative. In other words, the company matches you dollar for dollar. However, although there are both short-term benefits and long-term benefits in the corporate setting, you generally get full retirement benefits only at the end of your working life. In the marriage corporation, the conditions are remarkably different. First of all, because you immediately commit yourself to the union and pronounce the words "I do" during the wedding ceremony, which concomitantly means accepting Jesus Christ as your personal Lord and Savior, you start reaping the benefits. This is because you immediately gain a lifetime partner. You also gain a lifetime companion and helper, in accordance with God's pronouncement in Genesis 2:18, "It is not good for the man to be alone." This is further validated in the words of the preacher, in Ecclesiastes 4:9,10, "Two are better than one, because they have a good return for their labor: If either of them falls down, one can help the other up. But pity anyone who falls and has no one to help them up."

Also, as soon as you establish the marriage corporation, you have established the board of directors, with God as chairman, husband as president, and wife as executive vice president. What this automatically means is that you now have the added advantage of a direct line of communication with God, your chairman. What is more, you do not have to download any phone numbers, nor do you need any email addresses. Anytime you need to communicate with God, you simply open your mouth and speak. How would it not be so? It would be that simple because, as it states clearly in Psalm 127:1, "Unless the Lord builds the house, the builders labor in vain. Unless the LORD watches over the city, the guards stand watch in vain." Even more interesting, He is always close by. He lives in the house with you and your spouse. He is at the head of the table when you sit down for dinner. He is always only a prayer away.

Additionally, as soon as you commit to the union, you become fully vested in the marriage corporation, as distinct from what occurs at the workplace, where you become fully vested only after you have put in so many years of service to the company. Also, because you are fully invested at the start of your marriage journey by the simple virtue of committing yourself with the golden words "I do," you have automatically invested 100 percent into the union. Mathematically, this means that between you and your spouse, 200 percent is immediately invested, right from the first day, and then God matches the both of you with His own 200 percent. You now have 400 percent invested benefits to play around with. Can you beat that? What is more, every bit of that 400 percent is available to each of you in the course of your marital journey together, for the simple and equally fascinating mathematical fact that in God's marriage corporation, one plus one equals one! Can you now see why cohabitation, for instance, is totally valueless? In cohabitation's language of the flesh, which, sadly, is also the language of a marriage not solidly built in accordance with God's prescribed covenant, each partner brings in only 50 percent and waits for the other person to bring in another 50 percent, bringing the total to 100 percent. In cohabitation, God does not match this with anything. Can you blame Him? He does not recognize the union in the first place! In the corporate world, at least the management matches you with whatever percentage you can put in by the time you retire. So, even if you achieved 100 percent contribution, the company matches it with 100 percent, and you have 200 percent. Compare that with the 400 percent of the marriage corporation. I recall a conversation I had with a lady at a recent convention. She told me that, in her marriage, her husband brings in 50 percent, and she brings in 50 percent, and so between them they bring in 100 percent. I found that somehow strange, because I was wondering what happened to each person's other 50 percent. In the marriage corporation, we come in as total individuals who are supposed to pour in our total selves of 100 percent each to create a oneness. In other words, what each person brings is the entire personal package of commitment, body, and even finances with absolutely nothing held back. That is what I mean by a contribution of 100 percent. When you are bringing in 50 percent, you are obviously holding something back. In our marriage, Nephetina and I have brought in our 100 percent each so that God can match our combined 200 percent in the benefits that accrue to us. I think it's also possible that the concept of fifty-fifty love, as has been popularized by romantic fiction, may be misleading people into the belief that only a cumulative of 100 percent is achievable in anything. But we know that this is not strictly true, don't we? We know that there can be as many multiples of 100 percent in anything we wish to achieve in this world, and it is certainly so in the marriage corporation, where a peak-performing marriage actually receives a total of 400 percent benefit package during the course of its existence.

Another great benefit of early and full investment into your marriage is that you can reap full benefits of God's special grace to survive the trials and tribulations of marriage when they come calling. It is inevitable that these times of trial and tribulation will come. That is not negotiable. What is of paramount importance is how you weather the storm. A couple that is not fully invested through a one hundred-one hundred investment package will be less likely to survive such storms than a couple that has done so right from the beginning of the marriage. This is also a remarkable benefit of the marriage corporation. The greater your investment, the greater the returns on your investment. This is an immutable law of business. It is also an immutable law in the boardroom of the marriage corporation, especially if you also invest in God, the chairman of the board. The more you invest in Him, the more He will invest in you. How do you invest in God? You do this through prayers, offerings, and service to others, in full recognition that good deeds come from God. Also, the more you invest in God, the more He provides you with the tools to tackle the challenges of your marriage when arise. Additionally, He will show us in what areas of our marriage on which to focus our investment efforts before they fester into open sores. We all have weaknesses in the fabric of our marriages, and it is important for us to be able to periodically visit these areas and mend them.

God's blueprint for the marriage corporation contains policies and procedures. Now, what are these policies and procedures?

Contrary to what a lot of people believe, similar as the two terms may appear, they are quite distinct and are not mutually interchangeable in usage. A policy is a broad guideline for action, while a procedure is a relatively detailed set of instructions for carrying out specific actions. Therefore, a procedure would be a description of actions that would be carried out in line with an established policy. At this stage, it may be pertinent to give an example that highlights the distinction between a procedure and a policy. For instance, in some companies, the employees are obligated to periodically file a report on the number of hours they have worked and submit same to the accounts department in the form of an invoice. Now, this is where procedure takes over. Usually, the company issues a set of instructions on how the report should be filed, and these include how to present the information, what information to include, the expected content, the person to whom the information should be submitted, and the deadline for submitting the information. Generally, it is widely accepted that procedures will be updated much more frequently than policies, which are invariably set over long periods of time. It is also widely acknowledged that a company is simply asking for trouble if it fails to disseminate policies and procedures in a proper manner, as such a situation would lead to corporate chaos in the day-to-day operations of its business. By the same token, if the couple in a marriage corporation are not in full possession of the relevant instructions delivered in the proper manner, they cannot exploit the full benefits promised by God. This is also why the pastors and elders of the church must be the epitome of spiritual integrity, as any obvious violations of the instructions on their part will amount to imparting the instructions in an improper manner, which can lead the members of the church astray. Additionally, as the Bible says in James 2:14, "What good is it, my brothers and sisters, if someone claims to have faith but has no deeds? Can such faith save them?" We build our faith by hearing the Word of God. So, we build our faith by going to church to fellowship and to take part in Bible studies and other church activities, as all these activities provide a platform for God's instructions to be imparted to us.

These instructions should be very clear to singles before they enter into the marriage covenant. Premarital counseling should involve getting them very familiar with the instructions in the Bible about the marriage corporation. After all, if you are going to attend an interview for a job placement at a particular company, you are more than likely to have done intensive research on that company. You likely know how long it had been in existence, its corporate culture, and a host of other relevant information that would encourage you to take a job with them. The same logic applies to the marriage corporation. A prospective couple ought to know in detail what they are going into. They ought to know that they are about to make a lifelong commitment. Most people realize only too well that marriage is a very deep commitment, and that is what scares a lot of people away from it. But if they are properly counseled on the vast benefits that are accruable because of their union, they will be more inclined to make a covenant decision.

An employee handbook is a document that carries a lot of legal responsibility. In fact, if it is proved that an employee was not issued the handbook, he or she is not liable in case of breach of job protocol. The employee cannot even be fired. As a matter of fact, even when there are updates in company policies and procedures, usually employees are supposed to sign off that they have read such updates and fully understand them. In the church, a pastor imparts God's instructions to the members. We all know that sometimes the wrong instructions are given, or perhaps wrong examples are set for the members. The truth is that the instruction manual, the Bible, is accessible to everyone, and it becomes our responsibility to always study the Word of God so that we can personally confirm what we are being taught. That is why the Bible itself asks us to be discerning in the acquisition of knowledge. Ignorance of the contents of the Bible is never an excuse from seeking righteousness. The Kingdom of God is readily available to anyone who actively seeks it. Therefore, the instruction manual must be studied and understood. Just as the company can fire you, so can God fire you! How does God fire you? Simple. He takes His grace away from you. He removes His umbrella of protection from over your head, leaving you open to just about anything, especially the machinations of the devil. You become totally vulnerable, and anything can happen to you. One thing is clear. If a company sets out its policies and procedures in a clear and totally lucid manner, it keeps its employees from flouting its rules and regulations. God's instruction manual is the Bible. The Bible is very clear about God's instructions. It is a complete book. If one follows the instructions concerning marriage very carefully, one can only reap its benefits.

In a company, if as an employee you make an unauthorized withdrawal of money from your retirement plan, you get penalized for it. The corollary in the marriage corporation is that if you make an early withdrawal through infidelity, which can lead to divorce, you can be severely penalized. In fact, the penalty is so severe that it adversely affects parents, children, and the community. Worse, especially when divorce comes into the picture, some people never fully recover from the effects of unfaithfulness and divorce, and even when they seemingly do, they carry the effects into their next marriage, thereby creating a vicious cycle in their lives. This is why early withdrawal is not an option for God's people in The Marriage Corporation. The effects on others and on the community are simply too enormous. A covenant is a promise, and God's covenant with us in the marriage corporation is that He will give us a protective cover. When we make these sort of early withdrawals, He removes this cover, and we are left open to any of a wide variety of terrible things, which can even include suicide.

In conclusion, we should note that there are some actions that can fetch us penalties, and we should avoid them. These include, but are not limited to, not engaging in conscientious fellowship with God and flirting with members of the opposite sex. A lot of married people continue to act as if they are still single. They seem to conveniently forget that they now wear a wedding ring. Also, refusing to be openly honest with one's spouse, not spending quality time with the family, deceitfulness, engaging in negative thoughts about one's spouse, and not attending to one's responsibilities in the home, which translates to not taking care of one's department in the home, are all things that can detract from accessing the benefits of the marriage corporation. A man, for instance, must continue to proactively be the leader of his home, and abdication of this spiritual responsibility can spell danger for the integrity of the marriage corporation.

Finally, you must continue in good faith what you have started. For instance, if a man started dating his wife and was very attentive to her, listened warmly to her whenever she wanted to express herself, took her out to romantic dinners, and generally was a very good friend to her, he must continue with all those activities when he is married, so that the benefits of the marriage corporation can continue to be yours to claim.

The policies and procedures of God should continually be our guiding compass as we run the affairs of our marriage corporation, and His Word is sufficient unto us in relevant regard. In Jeremiah 29:12, He says, "Then you will call on me and come and pray to me, and I will listen to you." In Philippians 3:3, 4, He admonishes us thus, "Do nothing out of selfish ambition or vain conceit. Rather, in humility value others above yourselves; not looking to your own interests but each of you to the interests of the others." In Ephesians 5:25, He says, "Husbands, love your wives, just as Christ loved the church and gave himself up for her." Finally, in 1 Peter 4:8, God says, "Above all, love each other deeply, because love covers over a multitude of sins."

To Him be all the glory. Amen.

Reflections

1. You do not really have a marriage corporation until you are marriedinChrist.
2. In the marriage corporation, your pastor is the human resources person who hand you the Bible, which is your employee handbook.
3. Unlike in the corporate setting, where you get your benefits at the end of your working life, in the marriage corporation you immediately make the commitment and gain the benefits of a lifetime partner, a lifetime companion, and a helper.
4. As soon as you make the commitment, you gain a direct line of communication to God.
5. As soon as you make the commitment, you become fully vested in the marriage corporation, and God matches your investment fully.

6. As soon as you make the commitment, you can reap full benefits of God's special grace to survive the trials and tribulations of marriage through your one hundred-one hundred investment package.
7. God's blueprint for the marriage corporation is contained in policies and procedures that the pastor will deliver.
8. The penalties for flouting the rules of the marriage corporation can be severe indeed.

~12~

The Serrano's Testimony

Two are better than one, because they have a good return for
their labor: If either of them falls down, one can help the other
up. But pity anyone who falls and has no one to help them up.

—Ecclesiastes 4:9–10

Throughout this thirty year journey of our marriage, we have
certainly had our share of struggles and challenging times.
However, the benefit of understanding our individual and joint
responsibilities within a covenant marriage as God designed it,
as well as our roles as presented in *The Marriage Corporation*,
has been of tremendous help. We have overcome many obstacles
along the way. We realized and accepted early in our marriage that
we did not yet have a clear understanding of the roles we should
play within our relationship. After seeking out wise counsel in
a mutual effort to gain better understanding of each other, we
acknowledged that we truly needed and wanted some help. Upon
obtaining counseling, we were able to communicate with each
other much better. The result was that the desire to give up faded
as we journeyed on together, triumphing over life's difficult blows
and sometimes unpredictable downfalls.

Counseling gradually became neutral ground and a place of adventure where we explored and learned the other person's heartfelt concerns, likes, and dislikes. Counseling became not only a place of reckoning, but also a sort of boardroom that helped us sort through and sum up our differences, allowing us not only to communicate better, but also to grow closer and begin to have mutual understanding. We worked through challenges, came up with solutions, and remained determined to do better. Initially, we did not have a Christian counselor, but rather received great tools that we used throughout our relationship and still use today. Such tools include the book *The Five Love Languages* by Gary Chapman. This book helped us learn our mate's desire for love, and as we understood each other's love language, we began to respond differently by meeting each other's needs. Such tools showed us how to shut others out and have date nights once a week that we devote to spending quality time together. These things ultimately taught us how to consider the other person speaking by showing understanding when communicating. They came in handy when we found ourselves in a new situation that was almost unimaginable and that almost ruined our marriage of twenty-four years at that time. Yes, even after pushing a quarter of a century together, we were still caught off guard by the enemy and hit with a blow of trickery that almost wiped us out. We were then referred to a Christian counselor who has been a lifeline in our marriage ever since. We share this with you so that you can understand that, firstly, you are not alone; secondly, God has not forgotten you; and thirdly, this thing called marriage is a journey of good, bad, and sometimes ugly. The marriage corporation takes strategy for it to work. You must work together at being intentional to succeed in marriage. Remember, you are God's design and handiwork, and you were built for this.He never intended for you to fail. God equipped each of us with everything we need to be successful in our marriages.

It is our sincere hope that some of the corporate strategies you have read in this book are already making you consider your own action plan going forward. Begin to consider what your forever looks like or what you desire it to look like. You should always be looking to be better as a couple, better as a husband, and better as a wife. Both of you are only too human. Because of this, it is only natural that, even if only on the subconscious level, you will expect to be rewarded for your efforts at working for the success of your marriage. The good thing is that God, the chairman of your marriage corporation, has put a reward plan in place right from day one of your marriage. First of all, when you commit yourself to the union and pronounce the words "I do" at your wedding, you start benefiting from His reward plan. What are the components of this plan? You immediately gain a lifetime partner. You also gain a lifetime companion and helper in accordance with God's pronouncement in Genesis 2:18, "It is not good for the man to be alone." This is further explained by the preacher in Ecclesiastes 4:9,10, "Two are better than one, because they have a good return for their labor: If either of them falls down, one can help the other up. But pity anyone who falls and has no one to help them up." Secondly, as soon as you commit to the union, you become a full investor in the marriage corporation, and because you are fully invested at the start of your marriage journey through the utterance of the magic words "I do," you have automatically invested 100 percent into the union, and every bit of your joint cumulative investment with your spouse becomes available to each of you in the course of your marital journey together. The currency of the dividends of this investment is found in the joy, bliss, contentment, and fulfillment of your marital union. Thirdly, you will start reaping the full benefits of God's special grace to survive the trials and tribulations of marriage when they come calling. It is inevitable that these times of trial and tribulation will come. That is not negotiable. What is of paramount importance is how you are able to weather the storms, as we have weathered ours.

Our Christian counselor always helped us to go back to the source for answers. Well, our source is the one who created us and instituted this thing called marriage. As we read the material given to us by our counselor, we were now face-to-face with God by way of His holy Word called scripture in a book called the Bible. In the scriptures, we were shown Christ as the head of the church, as it says in Ephesians 5:23 (KJV). Not that this was our first time seeing this, as were both have ministry work we are doing for the Lord, but it was as if we were reading these scriptures for the first time. God's Word began to illuminate from the pages and into our hearts. We learned what the role of a husband is, which ultimately is to love his wife and lead her by example, especially one of serving and making decisions. Yes, husbands are to love their wives as Christ loves the church (Ephesians 5:25). We were shown what the role of a wife is. "Wives submit yourselves unto your own husband as unto the Lord." (Ephesians 5:22). In accepting our roles, we began to see and understand the need for order and for structure in marriage. In addition, this has given us our foundation for writing this book, and that foundation is the understanding that everything in and about marriage begins and ends with God.

We pray that this book will prove to be an invaluable tool that you will use at the appointed time as you walk together in agreement while continuing on your journey to forever in your marriage, thereby obtaining the ultimate success— "till death do you part"!

Printed in the United States
By Bookmasters